BE FRIENDS
OF GOD

Also by John Leinenweber

Love One Another, My Friends:
St. Augustine's Homilies on the
First Letter of John

BE
FRIENDS
OF GOD

Spiritual Reading from
Gregory the Great

In An English Version
By John Leinenweber

COWLEY PUBLICATIONS
Cambridge, Massachusetts

Published in the United States of America by
Cowley Publications, a division of the Society of St. John
the Evangelist. No portion of this book may be reproduced,
stored in or introduced into a retrieval system, or transmitted,
in any form or by any means including photocopying without
the prior written permission of Cowley Publications, except
in the case of brief quotations embodied in
critical articles and reviews.

International Standard Book Number: 1-56101-009-X
Library of Congress Number: 90-35274

Cover and interior illustrations by Helen Siegl

Library of Congress Cataloging-in-Publication Data
Gregory I, Pope, ca. 540–604.
[Sermons. English. Selections]
Be friends of God : spiritual reading from Gregory the Great
/ in an English version by John Leinenweber.
p. cm.
ISBN 1-56101-009-X (alk. paper)
1. Spiritual life—Catholic authors. I. Leinenweber, John. II. Title.
BX2349.G69313 1990
248.4'814—dc20   90-35274

This book is printed on acid-free paper and was produced in the
United States of America.

Cowley Publications
980 Memorial Drive
Cambridge, Massachusetts 02138

To the monks of
Saint Gregory's Abbey, Portsmouth,
and of
Saint Gregory's Abbey, Downside.

ACKNOWLEDGMENTS

As a Benedictine novice in the late 1950s I studied excerpts from Saint Gregory's homilies, which we sang at Vigils along with those of Augustine, Ambrose, and the others. Some of these remained in my memory during all the intervening years, when readings in English by a greater variety of writers were introduced.

In 1988 I was asked by Cistercian Publications to give an editorial review to Dom David Hurst's English translation of the complete collection of gospel homilies of Gregory the Great, which has been published as *Gregory the Great: Forty Gospel Homilies*. The idea came to me then that many lay people and clergy might also benefit from a devotional reading of Saint Gregory. Consequently, I went through the homilies again and selected passages that interested or moved me. These passages I revised, attempting to make them sound as if they might have been delivered in our own times, and grouped them according to some broad themes. My confrère at the Hermitage of the Dayspring, Brother Aelred Seton Shanley, made many suggestions as to ways I could make Gregory speak more plainly to a modern reader. Cynthia Shattuck of Cowley Publications helped with the organization of the volume and provided welcome encouragement.

I offer this book to the monks of St. Gregory's Abbey, Portsmouth, Rhode Island, and St. Gregory's Abbey, Downside, in England. Both monasteries were my home at different times. It is dedicated also to the memory of Dom Gregory Borgstedt, who possessed many of the qualities we find in his namesake and shared them generously with his brothers in the monastery and his friends.

John Leinenweber

CONTENTS

COMMUNITY

THE INCARNATION

REDEMPTION

LAST THINGS

HOMILY INDEX   187

BIBLICAL INDEX   199

PREFACE

I first met John Leinenweber in 1965 while on re-
treat at Mt. Saviour Monastery, Elmira, New
York. That initial visit proved to be the beginning of a friendship both with the Mt. Saviour community and with Brother John which continues to be
a source of much joy and strength.

Over the years Brother John's thorough grasp of
the monastic tradition together with his keen ability
to relate it to the world and the struggles of
humankind have made him a wise guide not only to
me but to many others as well.

As an experienced practitioner of the Benedictine
discipline of *lectio*, or meditative reading, Brother
John's counsel often takes the form of recommended
reading, running all the way from ancient homilies to
contemporary psychology.

I am therefore very grateful to him for these selections from the homilies of Gregory the Great, which
are offered to present day Christians as the enduring
word of one of the early sons of St. Benedict who,
like us, lived in difficult and unsettling times.

Frank T. Griswold
Bishop of Chicago

BE FRIENDS
OF GOD

INTRODUCTION

Saint Gregory the Great, who was arguably one of the most significant figures in western history for the thousand years following his death, presided as bishop of Rome from 590 to 604 C.E. His great-grandfather was Pope Felix III, and Gregory himself was born into a wealthy and distinguished Roman family. But this was a Rome that had been sacked four times within a century and a half, and besieged four times in twenty years, a city that had suffered from pillage, fire, earthquake, floods, and plague.

In 568 the Lombards crossed the Alps, and three years later this barbarian horde came dangerously close to Rome. Gregory, who was about thirty years old, was then holding the office of prefect, the highest civic office in the city, with responsibility for finances, policing, and defense. Two years later he renounced his possessions, founded six monasteries on family property in Sicily, and retired into his own house on the Coelian Hill in Rome, which he turned into a monastery dedicated to Saint Andrew. But Gregory's period of monastic retirement was short, as Pope Benedict I made him a deacon of the Roman church, and in 578 or 579 Pope Pelagius II sent him as papal representative to the court of Tiberius II in Constantinople, then the capital of the Byzantine

Empire. Gregory must have found its magnificence a striking contrast to the ruins of Rome. He remained in Constantinople for a number of years without learning Greek, living with monks from his monastery in Italy.

In about 586 Pelagius recalled Gregory to Rome, where he resided in his monastery of Saint Andrew for the next few years. After the flooding of the Tiber was followed by an outbreak of the plague in Rome, Pelagius died in January 590 and Gregory was unanimously chosen to succeed him. He seems to have thought of fleeing in order to follow his inclination to contemplative life, but the emperor in Constantinople confirmed his election. Putting aside his own preference, he was consecrated as bishop of Rome in the Basilica of Saint Peter on 3 September 590. He served as pope—a title still used by popes, "Servant of the servants of God," is attributed to Gregory—until his death in 604.

With Gregory's election began, in the words of Edward Gibbon's *Decline and Fall of the Roman Empire*, one of the most "edifying" periods in church history. In the absence of other leaders, Gregory became the ruler of both civil and ecclesiastical Rome, and, one may say, of the West, owing to the traditional prestige of Rome as well as to his enormous administrative abilities. His influence was significant in moral and ascetical theology, church music and liturgy, ecclesiastical and civil administration, monasti-

cism, evangelization, and social welfare. Gregory con-
solidated the patrimony of Saint Peter (the lands
controlled by the papacy), laid the foundations for
temporal papal authority, and did much to establish
the idea that the papacy was the supreme authority in
the church. He thought that the patrimony of Peter
ought to be at the disposal of the church and of the
poor. Finally, he was responsible for appointing
Augustine (later the first archbishop of Canterbury)
and forty monks to establish a mission in England; in
less than two years they had baptized the king of Kent
with ten thousand of his Anglo-Saxons.

Gregory's writings have been succinctly characterized by a recent student of his spiritual teaching.[†]
His exegetical works on Job, Ezekiel, the Song of
Songs, and I Kings "were directed largely to monastic
audiences [and] each is a serious and sophisticated effort to marshal the learning of the past and open new
frontiers of spiritual knowledge." In contrast, the
Dialogues and Homilies on the Gospel are "works of a
more popular spirit. Filled with clear directives and
comforting miracles, they teach his audience more ef-
fectively than mere instruction and seem to express
the side of Gregory known for learned ignorance,"

[†] Carole Straw, *Gregory the Great: Perfection in Imperfection* (Berkeley,
CA: University of California Press, 1988), p. 6.

that is, for a wisdom acquired otherwise than from books. (Gregory describes Saint Benedict, at the time he left his studies in Rome with the intention of becoming a monk, as "knowingly ignorant and wisely unlearned.") The Pastoral Rule is a manual for bishops, but is useful to anyone exercising authority. And the eight hundred and fifty-four letters remaining are of great interest for the information they provide us of Gregory's character and his multifarious activities.

The selections that follow are drawn from Gregory's Homilies on the Gospel. In a prefatory letter printed in the Benedictine edition he tells his correspondent that he has preached forty homilies on the gospel lessons read according to custom in his church on certain days. Half of these he dictated, and the scribe then read them in the presence of the congregation; the other half he himself delivered before the congregation, and they were taken down as he spoke. "But certain brothers," he says, "burning for the sacred word, copied them before I had made the necessary small corrections." He likens these brothers to people who eat their food before it is fully cooked! His correspondent is not to allow these earlier copies to remain uncorrected.

The Benedictine editors note the place where each homily was delivered (the Roman basilicas of St. Peter—the Constantinian church that was replaced by the present great church in the sixteenth century—St. Felicity, St. Stephen, and so on), and the solemnity, Sunday or saint's day, when they can iden-tify them. Typically, following the text of the day's gospel, Gregory explains any difficulties he thinks his listeners may have in understanding the literal sense. Thus in the first of the homilies (delivered in St. Peter's on the Second Sunday of Advent, year un-known), on Luke 21:25-32, Gregory informs them of disasters which confirm the Lord's predictions, and explains the "powers of heaven" and what is meant by "lift up your heads."[†] Christians are to rejoice at the approach of the end of the world. "The world is not our friend," he tells his congregation, and quotes James 4.4. The disasters they hear of and see happen-ing around them are signs of the world's old age. He asks why they would love what they see cannot exist much longer, and quotes 1 John 2:15.

Following these moral admonitions, Gregory frequently illustrates his points by stories, some of which also appear in the Dialogues. The miraculous elements in them are so abundant and so naïve that many readers have had difficulty in believing that they were set down by the man who elsewhere shows such sound judgment and common sense. Only two of

---

[†] See selections 67 and 68.

Gregory's stories appear in this collection, those of the brother who repented and the monk Martyrius.[†]

Edward Gibbon writes of Gregory, "He frequently ascended the pulpit, and kindled, by his rude though pathetic eloquence, the congenial passions of his audience: the language of the Jewish prophets was interpreted and applied; and the minds of a people depressed by their present calamities were directed to the hopes and fears of the invisible world." In the selections from his homilies on the gospel which make up this book, one will find him preaching faith, patience, love of neighbor and especially of a poor neighbor (and this out of self-interest), loyalty, contempt for the good things of this life (he saw how little they could be depended on) and desire for those of the next, fear of the final judgment and hope of the reward promised for a good life.

Gregory was immersed in the teachings of Augustine, but lacked his speculative bent. In his character were mingled energy and reserve, idealism and practicality, asceticism and the desire for power. His health was bad, his longing for contemplative life was frustrated while his life as pope was a continual labor of preaching and the enforcement of discipline. Around him he could see calamities of every kind,

---

[†] See selections 66 and 18.

prodigies of nature, human cruelty. When all the institutions of society seemed to be collapsing, and people believed that the world was coming to an end, Gregory taught that there is order in the world. The net of the Christian faith takes in fish of all kinds, and we cannot now distinguish the good from the bad; but on the shore (at the end of time) the good will be kept and the bad thrown away. God rewards the good and punishes the wicked; our wickedness may be only to neglect to do the good we are able to do, as was the case with the rich man who never saw Lazarus sitting at his gate.

The Scriptures, Gregory reminds us, show us clearly enough how we can live good lives. We are to love as Jesus loved, imitating him even as he asked forgiveness for those who crucified him. And we are never to despair of God's mercy. We have only to repent, like Peter, like Zacchaeus, like the sinful woman who washed Jesus' feet with her tears. Gregory seems to have felt a deep sympathy with this woman, whom early writers identified with Mary Magdalene and Mary the sister of Lazarus. The sacred writers foretold all that was happening, and this ought to make us confident that their unfulfilled predictions will take place. From this Gregory drew his desire and hope for the joys of eternal life.

In his introduction to an English translation of Saint Athanasius's treatise on the Incarnation, C. S. Lewis addresses the question of why someone should read these old writings when there are plenty of modern works on the same subjects. In his reply Lewis advises readers to read one old book for every new book, or, if that is too much, one for every three new books. We all live in a given historical period, and historical periods are characterized by what "everyone knows" to be true. The old authors give us an opportunity of stepping outside of our own era, of considering other viewpoints, of broadening our horizons, of liberating our minds from the tyranny of the present. Lewis's challenge requires the effort of entering into the spirit of the old book, the effort to become free of commonly held opinions for the purpose of looking at them afresh. No one would claim that Gregory's opinions, in contrast to those of our own time, are all true or relevant, but on many matters he is well worth listening to. As Lewis says, "People were no cleverer then than they are now; they made as many mistakes as we. But not the same mistakes."

Two of Gregory's ideas in particular may seem like stumbling-blocks to a modern reader. First of all, he was very much aware that every one of us has an examination, a trial, a judgment, ahead of us. He is aware, too, that our Judge is not a pushover. The Judge frequently appears in Gregory's text as *districtus*, severe. The parables of judgment in Matthew 25 are never far below the surface of his mind. One may feel that we need the images of Jesus as the Good Shepherd, as the prodigal Father, as our brother, our friend, more today than we need the Son of man, sitting in judgment on his glorious throne. Gregory evidently saw the needs of the people of his time differently.

And that raises the second question. Did his hearers really need to be warned over and over again of the dangers of "earthly desires"? Was Gregory simply a spoil sport, a puritan, always afraid that someone, somewhere, might be enjoying something? Or did our Christian forebears experience the desires inspired by earthly, passing pleasures more powerfully than we do?

You may remember the section of the tenth book of Augustine's *Confessions* where he calls our response to the sensual appeal of food and drink, of sweet scents, of music, "the lust of the flesh which lies in the delight of our all senses and pleasures," and goes on to condemn "the mere itch to gain the knowledge and experience of...objects that are beautiful, clear-sounding, sweet-smelling, savory, soft to the touch," that is, the itch of curiosity. "What shall I say when, in my own house, a lizard catching flies, or a spider entangling them in her web, often holds my attention?" How are we to take this? Don't we feel a certain pleasure in the fact that a man of such intensity can pass an hour in so peaceful a way? And the tradition for which Augustine stands is perfectly aware of the danger of human beings thinking they can live like angels; it is a warm-blooded, not a cold, tradition.

It may be that to get Gregory's thought we need to substitute for "earthly desires" the word "addictions," meaning desires we cannot control, experiences we cannot live without, indulgences that harm rather than benefit us. Gregory expresses this idea in selection 30, "Love and Hate." Friendship was certainly as precious to the ancients as to ourselves, but Gregory recognizes that friendship with another human being may in some circumstances be an impediment to friendship with God. When that is the case, he is in no doubt as to what a Christian must do.

But short of that, experience has taught him that in the case of physical, earthly things, it is the desire that we enjoy and not its gratification. With spiritual things, although our desire is likely to be weak, the gratification is endlessly pleasurable (see selection 1, "Pleasure."). This is not a case of sour grapes: Gregory enjoyed a fine intelligence and all that wealth and power could give him. If he desired something else, it was because he found it more desirable.

Listening always invites a response. Old images of the holy teachers of the Church showed them listening to the Holy Spirit, in the form of a dove, and then writing down what they heard. Those who read their writings, or listened to their preaching, were then receiving from the Holy Spirit at only one remove. Those who had received the gift of teaching were passing on their gift (see the section entitled "Ministry").

Saint Benedict, whose life Gregory told in book two of the *Dialogues*, made reading a central part of monastic life. He assigned about four hours daily to *lectio divina*, or spiritual reading, and made it the chief occupation of Sundays. He had in mind something different from what we usually mean by "reading" today. Esther De Waal writes that lectio "is not to stop short at the acquisition of mere knowledge; above all it should form the basis of a continuing dialogue with Christ which will colour the actual quality and experience of daily living." In the spirit of lectio divina, "words are tasted to release their full flavour, weighed in order to sound the full depths of their meaning....The act of reading makes the reader become a different person; reading cannot be separated from living."[†]

I began working with original texts of some of the church fathers for my own spiritual reading, because I realized than when I approached them in English translation I did so with my habit of speed reading. Translating slows me down. There is a way in which modern printing techniques and the availability of

---

[†] Esther de Waal, *Seeking God: The Way of St. Benedict* (Collegeville, MN: Liturgical Press, 1984), pp. 147-48.

books does us a disservice. Earlier readers would have held handwritten books, the result of weeks or months of labor with pen and ink, on vellum, perhaps, or handmade paper. Sometimes the letters would have flowed in unbroken lines across the page, leaving the reader to decide where one word ended and another began, or where to make the sentence and paragraph breaks.

Reading under those conditions would have been something like working on a precious puzzle, and a phrase used by Saint Benedict makes this image seem particularly appropriate. *Vacare lectioni*, which appears six times in chapter 48 of the *Rule*, means to be free for reading because one has leisure, one has chosen to set aside a period of time when one will have no other occupation.[†] Nowadays people may feel guilty when they take time for nothing but a leisurely reading of some appealing text, yet a long tradition makes it one of the key elements of a spiritual life.

Reading texts such as those by Saint Gregory gathered in this volume requires a kind of freedom from the preoccupations as well as the presuppositions of daily life. It would be well for the reader to

---

[†] See Ambrose Wathen, "Monastic *Lectio*: Some Clues from Terminology," *Monastic Studies* 12 (1976): 207-215.

find a quiet place and a quiet time; though perhaps, as the readings are short, they could be used to fill an interval in an otherwise busy period. Gregory is a wise and discerning friend, able to bring out of the treasury of his experiences precious gifts to challenge and console us. His intention is not so much to give us answers as to change our lives.

DESIRE FOR GOD

KNOCK AND IT SHALL
BE OPENED TO YOU ✠
LK 11 · 9

1 ✦ PLEASURE

We are aware of a difference between the pleasure we experience in our bodies and that we experience in our hearts. Physical pleasures, when we lack them, arouse in us an all-consuming desire for them. As soon as we possess and devour them, though, our satisfaction turns into distaste. Pleasures of the spirit, on the other hand, seem distasteful when we do not possess them, but once they begin to be ours, our desire awakens. The more hungrily we seek them when we have begun to enjoy them, the more do we enjoy them even as we hunger for them. With our bodies it is the desire that gives us pleasure, not the gratification of our desires; with the spirit, as the desire is nothing, the fulfillment is all the more pleasing. Physical desire leads to satiety, and satiety leads to distaste for what we desired; spiritual desire produces satiety, and satiety leads to renewed desire.

The pleasure of the spirit increases our inner longing even while it satisfies us, since the more we savor it, the more we perceive that there is something more to long for. When we do not possess it, however, we cannot love it, because its savor is unknown. Who can love what is unknown? Therefore the psalmist counsels us, *Taste and see that the Lord is good.* He means that we will not get to know the Lord's goodness unless we taste it. You must taste the food of life with your hearts, so that by trying it you can become capable of loving its goodness.

Humanity lost this pleasure when it sinned in paradise. It left the garden unable to taste the food that is everlastingly good. We ourselves are born amid the hardships of exile. We have come to this place with a feeling of distaste. We do not know what we ought to desire. The more we distance ourselves from a share in that good food, the more does the disease which brings about our aversion to it increase. Now we have no desire for inner pleasure, since we have long been unaccustomed to tasting it. Our aversion consumes us, we are worn out by the long scourge of our starvation. Because of our inner unwillingness to taste the good things prepared for us, in our wretched outer state we have come to love our hunger.

But our loving God does not abandon us as we abandon him. He brings to our memory the pleasures we have spurned, and sets them before us. By a promise he lifts us from our lethargy, inviting us be rid of our aversion. That is what he means when he tells us the story beginning, A *certain man gave a great dinner and invited many*.

2 + THE TREASURE HIDDEN IN A FIELD

We say that the kingdom of heaven "is like" things of earth for this reason, my friends, that our minds may rise from the things they know to what they do not know; that they may be carried from something visible to what is beyond vision; that they may be ignited, so to speak, by what they have learned from experience, and set aglow; that they may learn from what they already know to love things both known and unknown.

Jesus compares the kingdom of heaven to a treasure hidden in a field. Someone finds this treasure and hides it, and in the joy of discovery, goes and sells everything he or she possesses and buys that field.

We should note that the treasure, once discovered, is hidden for protection's sake. It is not enough for us to stake our claim to the joy of heaven, guarding it from the forces of evil, if we do not also hide it from human praise. In this present life we are traveling on the road which will lead us to our homeland. Evil lies in wait along our route like a highway robber. Those who carry their treasure openly on the road are asking to be robbed.

I don't say this to prevent our neighbors from seeing our good works, since Jesus says, *Let them see your good works and glorify your Father in heaven*. It is so that we will not seek other people's praise for the good we do. We must do our work in the open, but in such a way that our motives remain hidden. This way we are an example to our neighbors by the good we do, and yet by the intention with which we are seeking to please God alone, we always choose what is secret.

The treasure the Lord speaks of is the desire for heaven, and the field in which the treasure is hidden is our zeal in pursuing heaven. Those people truly sell everything and buy the field who renounce the pleasures of the flesh and conquer their desire for the things of earth by the discipline of heaven. Then nothing their bodies value is agreeable to them any longer, and their spirits have no fear of physical death.

3 + THE PEARL OF GREAT VALUE

The kingdom of heaven is said to be like a merchant who is seeking fine pearls and finds one of great value. When he has found it, he sells everything and buys it. Those who know perfectly, as far as anyone can, the delight of the life of heaven, gladly abandon everything they have loved on earth. In comparison with what they have found, everything appears worthless. They abandon what they have, they give away the things they have accumulated. Their minds are set on fire by the things of heaven, and nothing earthly pleases them. Whatever earthly things used to please them by their beauty now appear hideous, because only the precious pearl gleams in their minds. Solomon justly says of such love that *love is stronger than death.* Just as death destroys the body, so an ardent desire for life in its fullness cuts them off from the love of anything less. It renders one it has perfectly taken hold of oblivious to earthly desires.

4 + JOY IN HEAVEN

We must consider, my friends, why the Lord says that there is more joy in heaven over converted sinners than over the righteous who have stood firm. But is this not what we experience every day? We often see people who aren't oppressed by any burden of sin. They remain firm in the path of righteousness, they do nothing that is forbidden—but neither are they filled with eager longing for their heavenly home. They allow themselves all that is allowed, since they are aware that they have done nothing forbidden. Frequently they are reluctant to do the highest good because their consciences are blissfully untroubled.

On the other hand, sometimes those who remember that they have done something wrong feel the sting of conscience, and their sorrow sets them on fire with the love of God. They practice extraordinary virtues, eagerly embrace all the difficulties of the struggle with the devil, abandon all the things of this world, flee honors, rejoice when they receive abuse, are on fire with desire and long expectantly for their heavenly home. Because they are aware that they have strayed from God, they compensate for earlier losses by later gains.

This is why there is more joy in heaven over a converted sinner than over a righteous person who has stood firm. A leader in battle has more love for a soldier who returns after he has fled, and who valiantly pursues the enemy, than for one who has never turned back, but who never acts valiantly. A farmer has greater love for land that bears fruit after having been cleared of thorns than for land that never had thorns, but never yielded a fruitful harvest.

Even so, let us know for sure that there are many upright people whose lives bring so much joy that it is hard to imagine that even repentant sinners could surpass them. Many are unaware of evil in themselves, yet they give themselves eagerly to suffering as if they had been bound by every kind of sin. They reject everything that is allowed them, they prepare themselves for the world's scorn, they don't choose anything that gives them pleasure, they despise all visible things and are on fire for what is invisible, they rejoice to weep, they humble themselves in every way, and they grieve over their sins of mind and heart as others do over their sinful actions. What should I say of those who humble themselves in repentance over their sins of thought, and are always upright in deed, except that they are at once righteous and repentant? If the repentance of the unrighteous over their past misdeeds causes such joy in heaven, we can infer how much joy it causes God when the upright humbly weep over themselves.

5 ✦ THE SEARCH FOR GOD

The church uses the words of the Song of Songs to speak of her spouse: *Upon my bed during the night I*

*sought him whom my soul loves; I sought him and did not
find him. I will rise and go about the city, through its
squares and streets; I will seek him whom my soul loves.*
In her failure to find him she repeats her words, saying again, *I sought him and did not find him.* But since
discovery is not long delayed if she does not abandon
her search, she says that *the watchmen who guard the
city found me. Have you seen him whom my soul loves?
Scarcely had I passed them by when I found him whom
my soul loves.*

We seek the one we love upon our beds when we
are filled with longing for our Redeemer during the
short periods of rest we are granted during this present life. We seek him during the night, because even
though our hearts are already watchful for him, our
eyes are still blinded. It remains for us who do not
find the one we love to rise and go about the city.
That means that we must travel about the church of
the chosen with an inquiring heart. We must seek
him through its squares and streets, making our way
through broad and narrow places alike, on the watch
to make inquiries if any traces of him can be found
there. The watchmen who guard the city, and who
find us as we search, are the holy fathers who guard
the church's orthodoxy. They come to meet our good
efforts, teaching us by their words and by their writings. Scarcely have we passed them by when we find
him whom we love.

Delay in their fulfillment increases our holy desires; if delay causes them to fail, they were not desires. All those who were able to attain God, our Truth, were on fire with love. David said, *My soul has thirsted for the living God: when shall I come and appear before the face of God?* And he counseled us to *seek his face continually.* The prophet Isaiah said, *My soul has yearned for you in the night, and my spirit within my breast will watch for you in the morning.* And the church says in the Song of Songs: *I have been wounded with love.* It is only right that a soul that has borne in its heart a wound of love caused by its burning desire should receive healing from the sight of the Physician.

The church goes on to say, *My soul melted when he spoke.* The hearts of those who do not seek the face of their Creator are hard because they remain cold. If they should begin to burn with desire for following the One whom they love, they run, since the fire of love has melted them. Desire makes them uneasy, and everything they used to enjoy now seems good for nothing. They can find pleasure in nothing besides their Creator. What once delighted them now becomes grievously oppressive. Their sadness remains unconsoled as long as they are not beholding the One they desire. Their hearts sorrow. Light itself is loathsome. Scorching fire burns away the rust of sin in their hearts, and their souls are inflamed, as if they were gold, because gold loses its beauty through use, but fire restores its brightness.

6 ✙ PERSISTENCE IN PRAYER

We must believe that our Savior's miracles were truly performed, and that they are revelations as well; his works show us one thing by their power, and tell us another mystically. We do not know the historical identity of the blind man who was sitting by the way-side as Jesus drew near to Jericho, but we know who it is he mystically represents. The blind man is the human race. Driven from the joys of paradise in our first parents, and ignorant of the brightness of divine light, our race experienced the darkness of rejection. Yet we are enlightened by the presence of our Redeemer, so that we can already behold the joys of inner light through our desire for them, and can direct our footsteps, our good works, in the way of life.

The blind man is described as *sitting by the wayside*, and also as *begging*. Jesus himself told us: *I am the way*. Those who are ignorant of the brightness of eternal light are blind. If they already believe in their Redeemer they are sitting by the wayside. If they believe, and acknowledge the blindness of their hearts, and if they beg to receive the light of truth, they are sitting by the wayside and begging. If any of you recognize the darkness of your blindness, if any of you understand that you lack the light of truth, then cry out from the bottom of your hearts, cry out with your thoughts, cry out *Jesus, Son of David, have mercy on me!*

And the people ahead rebuked him that he should be silent. What is meant by the people who are ahead as Jesus comes, if not the throng of our physical desires and the uproar caused by our vices? Before Jesus comes into our hearts they disturb our thoughts by tempting us, and they thoroughly muddle the words in our hearts as we pray. We often desire to turn to the Lord when we have committed some wrong. When we try to pray earnestly against the wrongs we have committed, images of our sins come into our hearts. They blur our inner vision, they disturb our minds, they overwhelm the sounds of our plea. *The people ahead rebuked him that he should be silent,* since before Jesus comes into our hearts the evils we have done rise up in our thoughts as images, and they throw us into confusion in the very act of praying.

But let us hear what the blind man, who was still unenlightened, did: *He cried out all the more, Son of David, have mercy on me!* As great as the tumult of our thoughts must be our eagerness to persist in prayer. The crowd opposes our crying out, but it is surely necessary that the more harshly our heart's voice is repressed, the more firmly it must persist, in order to overcome the uproar of forbidden thoughts and to break in on Christ's gracious hearing.

I believe that we all observe in ourselves what I am saying. When we turn our minds from this world to God, when we are converted to the work of prayer, the things we once took pleasure in doing come to us in our prayer. They make demands on us; they come as burdens now. Only with difficulty does holy desire banish the recollection of them from our hearts; the sorrows of repentance scarcely overcome their images.

And Jesus stopped and ordered the blind man to be brought to him. You see that the one who was passing by stopped! While we are suffering a riot of images in our prayer, we realize that Jesus is in some sense passing by; but when we persist ardently in prayer, Jesus stops and we take him to our hearts as he passes by. He restores light: God is fixed in our hearts, and the light we have lost is given back to us.

And Jesus asked the blind man, *What do you want me to do for you?* Was one who could restore light ignorant of what the blind man wanted? But God wants to be asked for what he already knows we will request and he will grant. He counsels us to be untiring in our prayers, and yet he says that *your Father knows what you need before you request it of him.* He questions us so that we may ask him, he questions us to rouse our hearts to prayer.

The blind man immediately said: *Lord, that I may see.* He didn't ask the Lord for gold, but for light. He set little store by anything but light. My friends, let us imitate him. Let us not ask the Lord for deceptive riches, or earthly gifts, or fleeting honors; let us ask the Lord for light. And let us not ask for light that is confined to one place, or limited by time, or that ends with the coming of night. Brute animals experience that kind of light just as we do. Let us ask for the light which we can see, and only the angels besides us, light without beginning or end!

The way to this light is faith. Jesus says to the blind man whom he is enlightening, *Receive your sight, your faith has saved you.*

At once he saw, and he followed him. Those people see and follow the Lord who know what is good, and behave accordingly; those see, without following him, who know what is good, but who refuse to do it. My friends, if we too acknowledge the blindness that is part of our pilgrimage here below, if we sit by the wayside by believing in the mystery of our Redeemer, if we ask light from our Creator by praying earnestly for it day after day, if we have been enlightened after our blindness by perceiving this light through our understanding, then let us follow with our deeds the Jesus we behold with our hearts. Let us ponder the way he lived; let us follow his path.

7 ✛ PETER AND ANDREW

You have heard, my friends, that at a single word Peter and Andrew left their nets and followed Jesus. They had not seen him perform any miracles yet, and they had not heard him saying anything about eternal recompense, but at a single command from the Lord they forgot all their possessions.

You may be thinking that these two fishermen possessed almost nothing, and so you ask how much did they have to give up? In this case, my friends, it's the natural feelings and not the amount that we have to weigh. Those who have kept back nothing for themselves have left a great deal; those who have abandoned everything, no matter how little it may be, have left a great deal. We are attached to what we have and hold on to it; we long for what we do not yet have and try to get it. When Peter and Andrew renounced their desire to possess, they gave up a great deal; along with their possessions they renounced even their craving to possess. Those who imitate them give up as much, then, as those who do not imitate them crave to possess.

Don't ever say to yourselves, when you think of people who have given up a great deal, "I want to imitate them, but I have nothing to give up." If you renounce your desires, you are giving up a great deal. No matter how little they may be, our external possessions are enough for God. He weighs the heart and not the substance, and measures the effort it costs us and not the amount we sacrifice to him. If we consider only the external substance, we see that these astute businessmen, Peter and Andrew, traded their nets and their boat for the fullness of life!

8 + ETERNAL PASTURES

I have other sheep that are not of this fold. I must bring them in too, and they will heed my voice, and there will be one fold and one shepherd. The Lord foresaw the redemption of us who come from outside his own people when he said that he was bringing in other sheep, too. You see it happening every day, my friends. It is as if he has made one fold from two flocks, by joining the Jewish and Gentile races together by belief in himself, as Paul testifies when he says: *He is our peace, who has made both one.*

When he chooses the guileless of both races for eternal life he is leading sheep into his own fold. He says again: *My sheep heed my voice. I know them and they follow me; I give them eternal life.* A little earlier he had called himself *the door of the sheep,* and said of them: *Those who enter by me will be saved; they will go in and out, and will find pasture.* They will go in to faith; they will go out from faith to vision, from belief to contemplation; they will find pasture in the everlasting refreshment of heaven.

The Lord's sheep will find pasture because whoever follows him with a guileless heart is nourished on pastures of unfading greenness. What are the pastures of these sheep but the eternal joys of an ever-green paradise? The pasture of the chosen is the countenance of God. When we see him perfectly, our hearts will be endlessly satisfied with the food of life. Those who have evaded the snares of passing pleasures will rejoice in those pastures with the fullness of eternity.

There we will find choirs of angels singing hymns, there the whole company of heavenly citizens. There we will find the delightful celebration of those returning from the sad labor of their exile, the far-seeing choir of prophets, the apostles who are our judges. There we will find the victorious army of the innumerable martyrs, as happy there as they were in torment here; there confessors whose constancy has received its reward; there faithful men whose strength was not softened by the pleasures of the world; there holy women who overcame the world; there children who surpassed their years by their conduct; there old men and women whom age weakened, but who did not lose their capacity for doing good.

My friends, let us seek this pasture! There we will share the joy of so many citizens. This festival is calling us! If a celebration was announced for the dedication of some church, and people were gathering, would we not rush off to be present at such a great occasion? All of us would be there! We would believe we had suffered a serious loss if we missed out on this celebration of general happiness. The rejoicing of the chosen citizens in heaven is going on even now. They all rejoice with one another at their gathering. Yet we are lukewarm in our love of eternity; no desire sets us on fire; we do not seek out so great a celebration. We are without these joys—and we think we are happy!

Let us enkindle our hearts, my friends, let our faith again grow warm in what it believes, let our desire for heavenly things take fire. So to love is to be already on the way. We should not let any adversity call us back from the joy of this inner festivity. No difficulty on their journey alters the desire of people wanting to reach some particular place. You must not let any seductive good fortune lead you astray: they are foolish travelers who see a pleasant meadow on their journey and forget where they are going. We must let our hearts yearn for our heavenly home with all our desire; let them seek nothing in this world which they must leave quickly. If we are truly sheep of the heavenly Shepherd, and are not arrested by any delight along the way, we shall be satisfied with the eternal pastures on our arrival there.

REPENTANCE

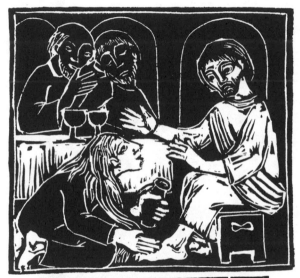

HER SINS ARE FORGIVEN
LK 7·47

Mary Magdalene had been *a sinner in the city.* She loved Jesus, the Truth, and she washed away with her tears the stains of her wickedness. Thus were the words of Truth fulfilled, that *her many sins have been forgiven her because she loved much.* She whose sins had kept her cold afterwards burned irresistibly with love. After she came to the sepulcher and failed to find the body of the Lord there, she believed that it had been taken away and reported this to the disciples. They came, and saw, and they believed that it was as the woman had said. It is written of them that *the disciples went back to the place where they had been,* and then it is said that *Mary stood outside the sepulcher weeping.*[†]

We must ponder Mary's state of mind. A great power of love inflamed her. When even the disciples departed from the sepulcher, she did not. She sought for him whom she had not found, weeping as she searched. Inflamed as she was by the fire of her love, she was burning with desire for the one she believed had been taken away. Thus it happened that she who stayed behind to seek him was the only one who saw

---

[†] Here, Gregory conflates three women: the sinful woman of Luke 7.36-50, the anointing woman of Matthew 26.7 and Mark 14.3 whom John (12.3) calls Mary, and Mary Magdalene.

him. Surely the essence of every good work is perseverance. Truth has told us that *the person who per-
severes to the end is the one who will be saved.*

Mary, *as she was weeping, stooped down and looked
into the sepulcher.* It is true that she had already seen
that the sepulcher was empty, and had already reported that the Lord had been taken away. Why did
she stoop down again, why did she want to look
again? It is never enough for a lover to have looked
once, because love's intensity does not allow a lover
to give up the search. Mary sought a first time and
found nothing; she persevered in seeking, and so it
happened that she found Jesus. It came about that her
unfulfilled desires increased, and as they increased
they embraced what they found.

Jesus said to her, Mary. First he had called her
"Woman," the common address at that time for one
of her sex, without being recognized. Then he called
her by her own name, as if to say: "Recognize him
who recognizes you." To Moses the Lord had said, *I
know you by name.* Moses was his own name. The
Lord told him that he knew him by name, as if saying
to him: "I do not know you in a general way, but particularly." Because Mary was called by name, she ac-
knowledged her Creator, and called him at once
Rabboni, which means Teacher. He was at once the
one she was outwardly seeking, and the one who was
inwardly teaching her to seek him.

10 + DIVINE COMPASSION

The sinful woman of the gospel is a witness to divine compassion. When the Pharisee wanted to keep her from the Lord he said: *If this man were a prophet he would surely know who and what sort of woman this is who is touching him, that she is a sinner.* But she had abandoned her promiscuity. She washed away the stains of her heart and body with her tears, and touched her Redeemer's feet. She sat at the feet of Jesus, and listened to his words. While he was alive she clung to him; later, when he was dead, she sought him, and found the dead man she was seeking alive. She found such favor with her Lord that it was she who was sent with his message to the apostles, who were themselves to be his messengers.

What should we see in this, my friends, except the boundless compassion of our Creator? God has put before us, as if for signs and examples of repentance, those restored to life through repentance after they fell. Think of Peter, of the thief, of Zacchaeus, of Mary—I see in them nothing else but examples of hope and repentance.

Some of you may have fallen away from the faith: look at Peter, who wept bitterly for his faint-hearted denial. Some of you may have been smouldering with malice and cruelty toward a neighbor: look at the thief, who even at the moment of his death reached the reward of life by repenting. Some of you may have been burning with greed and helped yourself to a stranger's goods: look at Zacchaeus, who if he had stolen anything from anyone restored it fourfold. Still others of you may have been on fire with lust and degraded yourselves: look at Mary, who purified her body with the fire of divine love.

See how our all-powerful God puts before us at every turn those whom we are to imitate. He provides examples of his compassion everywhere. Let us leave behind our taste for evil, even if we once savored it. Almighty God willingly forgets that we have done wrong; God is ready to count our repentance as innocence. If we have defiled ourselves since we were washed clean by the waters of salvation, let us be born again by our tears.

We must listen to our first pastor talk to us: *Like newborn children, desire milk!* We must return like little children to the breasts of our mother, the eternal Wisdom. We must drink from the bountiful breasts of the loving kindness of God. We must weep for our past misdeeds and shun those that lie ahead. Our Redeemer will solace our fleeting sorrows with eternal joy, he who lives and reigns with the Father in the unity of the Holy Spirit, God forever and ever.

11 ✛ SIGNS OF LOVE

Let us consider what a sign of his love it was for Jesus not only to allow the sinful woman to come into his presence, but even to allow her to touch his feet. Let us contemplate the grace of our merciful God, who looks on sinners and bears with us, putting up with those who resist him, and yet calling out gently every day through the gospel. God desires our confession from a pure heart, and forgives every fault we have committed.

Our Redeemer's mercy has mitigated for us the rigor of the Jewish Law. It is written there that if anyone does this or does that they shall be put to death, they shall be stoned. Our Creator appeared in the flesh, and it was not punishment he promised for the confession of sins, but life. He received a woman who confessed her wounds and sent her away healed. He altered the Law's harshness, preferring compassion; he mercifully set free those it justly condemned.

God intimated to us this promise of the compassion to come when he said through the prophet: *I do not will the death of a sinner, but that he be converted and live.* Again, it was said to every sinful soul under the figure of Judea, *If a man divorces his wife, and she leaves him and marries another man, will he return to her again? Will not that woman be polluted and defiled? You have prostituted yourself with many lovers: yet return to me, says the Lord.* God has given us the example of an immoral woman, and shows us that after her immorality her husband will not take her back. But God's compassion goes beyond this. God says that though her husband cannot possibly take back the prostituted woman, he himself is waiting for the prostituted soul, to take it back.

My friends, consider the import of such great love! God says that something cannot be done, and reveals that he himself can do it, against all custom. God calls out to those he declares defiled, he even seeks to embrace them; he complains that they have deserted him.

Do not squander this moment of mercy, do not throw away the medicine of love which has been offered us. Divine goodness calls us back when we have turned away; it prepares a lavish reception for us when we return. We must, all of us, consider our responsibility when God awaits us, when he is not vexed even when we have spurned him. Let those of you who would not stay with him return; let those who refused to remain upright at least get up after your fall.

Our Creator hints to us how great is his love with which he awaits us when he says through the prophet: *I have given heed and listened, but no one speaks what is good; there is no one who thinks again in his heart and says, What have I done?* We ought never to have thought of evil. But since we refused to think as we should, you see how he still bears with us in order that we may think again. Look at his great well of kindness, think of his merciful heart open wide to us. He is seeking those thinking again in the right way, whom he lost when they were thinking wrongly.

12 + REPENTANCE

When I think of Mary's repentance I am moved
more to weep than to speak. Who has so stony a
heart that this sinful woman's tears wouldn't soften
it? Remembering what she had done, she refused to
be moderate in what she was doing. She came in to a
house where people were dining; she came in unin-
vited; she poured out her tears while a feast was going
on. What grief so consumed her that she wasn't
ashamed to weep even during a feast? Her inner sense
of shame must have been so great that outwardly she
could be shameless!

What astonishes us more, my friends, Mary's coming or the Lord's accepting her? Should I say that he
accepted her, or that he drew her? I had better say
both, that he drew her and accepted her. I am sure
that he drew her interiorly with his mercy, and accepted her outwardly with his gentleness. But let us
see the way she was healed.

She brought an alabaster flask of ointment, and stand-
ing behind Jesus at his feet, she began to wet his feet with
her tears, and wiped them with the hair of her head, and
kissed his feet, and anointed them with the ointment. Isn't
it obvious, my friends, that the woman who had been
eager to do wrong had once used this ointment to
perfume her own body? What she had earlier used on
herself to her own disgrace she now offered to the
Lord. Her eyes once sought the world: now she wept,
chastising them by her repentance. She had used her

hair to compliment her face: now she used it to wipe away her tears. She had spoken proudly: now she kissed her Redeemer's feet. She found as many ways to offer sacrifice as she once had ways to offer pleasure. She converted her faults into virtues so that she could serve God in repentance as completely as she had rejected him in sin.

But on seeing this the Pharisee despised her. Censuring not only the sinful woman who had come in, but also the Lord who had accepted her, he said within himself: *If this man were a prophet, he would certainly know who and what sort of woman this is who is touching him, that she is a sinner.* The Pharisee's pride was true and his righteousness was false. He censured the suffering woman on account of her sickness, but he was suffering, too, from the wound of self-exaltation and did not know it. And he censured the physician for accepting her. The Pharisee was elated by his spurious righteousness and so he underestimated the seriousness of his illness.

As I say these things, I am painfully aware that some who have been entrusted with the priestly office, as I have been, despise those under their authority and spurn the sinners among the laity. They refuse to show compassion to those who confess their sins, and like the Pharisee, they scorn to be touched by a sinful woman. If this woman had approached the Pharisee's feet he would surely have driven her away. He would have believed he was being defiled by another's sin, since her true righteousness did not touch him.

When we see sinners, we must always weep for ourselves first. Perhaps we have fallen in the same way; or we can fall, if we haven't yet. And if the teaching office must eradicate vices by the power of discipline, we must nevertheless make a careful distinction: we must be uncompromising toward vice, but compassionate to human nature. If we have to punish sinners, we also have to sustain our neighbors. When our neighbors have abolished their wrong deeds by repenting, they are no longer sinners.

But let us see now the grounds on which the proud and arrogant Pharisee is found guilty. The Lord presents him with the example of two debtors. One owes less, the other more. When both have had their debts forgiven, the Lord asks, which of them has more love for the one who forgave them? He answers immediately that the one who was forgiven more loves more. The Pharisee is convicted by his own admission; he is like an idiot who carries the rope with which he will be bound!

Then the Lord recounts the sinful woman's good deeds, and what the so-called righteous man neglected to do: *I entered your house and you gave me no water for my feet, but she has wet my feet with her tears and wiped them with her hair. You gave me no kiss, but from the time I came in she has not ceased to kiss my feet. You did not anoint my head with oil, but she has anointed my feet with ointment.* Then he adds: *Therefore I tell you, her many sins are forgiven her because she has loved much.*

My friends, what do you think love is, if not fire? And what is sin, if not rust? Hence when he says that *many sins are forgiven her because she has loved much,* he means that she has completely burned away the rust of sin by the mighty flame of her love. The more a sinner's heart is consumed by the fire of love, the more fully is the rust of sin consumed.

The woman who came to the physician sick was healed, but there were others there who remained sick. At once those who were at table with him complained, saying within themselves, *Who is this who even forgives sins?* But the divine physician did not turn his attention to these others who were sick. He encouraged the woman he had healed by referring to her confidence in him, saying *Your faith has saved you; go in peace.* She had not doubted that she would receive what she asked for. Jesus bade her go in peace so that she would no longer be diverted from the road of truth.

13 ✦ THE KINGDOM OF HEAVEN SUFFERS VIOLENCE

From the days of John the Baptist until now the kingdom of heaven suffers violence, and the violent take it by force. Let us consider these words of our Christ very carefully. We must ask how the kingdom of heaven can suffer violence, who inflicts violence in heaven, and why, if the kingdom of heaven is able to suffer violence, it has endured it only since the days of John the Baptist?

When the Law says that if anyone does this or that they will surely die, it is obvious to everyone who reads it that all transgressors were struck with severe punishment, and that the Law did not restore them to life through repentance. Yet when John the Baptist came as forerunner of our Redeemer's grace, he preached repentance so that sinners who were dead as a result of their sins might be converted and live. Truly, then, from his days the kingdom of heaven has suffered violence. What is the kingdom of heaven but the place where the righteous live? The reward of a home in heaven is owed only to the righteous; the humble, the pure, the meek, and the merciful attain the joys of heaven. When those who have become swollen with pride, who have slipped into sins of the flesh or been inflamed with anger, or who must take blame for their cruelty, turn to repentance after they have sinned and receive eternal life, it is as if they enter a strange and unfamiliar place. What has John done by proclaiming repentance to sinners except to teach that violence is done to the kingdom of heaven?

My friends, let us think over the evils we have done, let us present ourselves before God with sorrow. By repentance we can seize the inheritance of the righteous, which we do not deserve by our way of life. God, the all-powerful, longs to suffer this kind of violence from us. He longs for us to seize the kingdom of heaven, which we have done nothing to deserve, by our tears. We must not let the nature of our wickedness, or its extent, break our hope.

Let the good thief show us the confidence we can have in pardon. He was not good because he was a thief, since his cruelty led him to that. His confession of guilt made him good. Think how incomprehensible is the mercy of our all-powerful God! The thief was caught red-handed in his thievery and hanged on a cross. There he confessed his guilt, there he was forgiven, there he was found worthy to hear Jesus say to him: *Today you will be with me in paradise.* How can we begin to describe God's great goodness? How can we begin to value it? From a criminal's punishment, the thief came to the prize for virtue!

Almighty God has allowed his chosen to succumb to certain sins. This is so that he may restore hope of forgiveness to others, who are under sin's domination, if they will only rise up to him wholeheartedly: for then God can open up for them the way to heaven through sorrow and repentance. Let us then embrace sorrow, let us rid ourselves of our sins by tears and *fruits worthy of repentance.* We must not squander the time that has been granted us. We see so many freshly washed clean of the wrongs they have done: what else

do we have in them except a pledge of the compassion from on high?

WORKS OF
LOVE

THE GREATEST WILL BE
THE ONE WHO SERVES
THE REST ✝ MT 23·11

S ince all of Christ's statements contain commandments, why does he say of love, as if it were something special, *This is my commandment, that you love one another?* He says this because every commandment is about love, and all of them add up to one commandment. Whatever he commands is founded on love, just as the many branches of a tree come from one root. The branches, which are our good works, are lifeless unless they remain attached to the root of love.

It follows that our Lord's commandments are both many and one. They are many because there is a variety of good works, and they are one in their root, which is love. He himself often teaches us in the gospel how we are to practice this love. He tells us to love our friends in him, and our enemies for his sake. Those who love their friends in God and their enemies for God's sake possess true love.

Many people love their neighbor because of some blood relationship or with affection that is purely natural, and Scripture does not oppose this kind of love. But what we give freely and naturally is one thing, and what we give in obedience to the Lord's commandment is another. These people indisputably love their neighbor, but they don't attain the sublime reward of love since their love comes from a natural and not from a spiritual motive.

And so when the Lord said, *This is my command-ment, that you love one another*, he added immediately, *just as I have loved you*. He means that we must love for the same reason that he has loved us.

My friends, when the devil draws us to take pleasure in passing things, he also stirs up a weak neighbor against us. This neighbor may plot to take away the very things we love. In this case, our enemy is not concerned with doing away with our earthly possessions; he wants to destroy our love. We may suddenly begin to burn with hatred, and while we try to be outwardly invulnerable, inwardly we are gravely wounded. As we defend our few external possessions we lose our great interior one, because when we love something passing we lose true love. Anyone who takes away one of our external possessions is an enemy; if we begin to hate this enemy, our loss is not of anything external, but of something inside our-selves. And so whenever we suffer anything from a neighbor, we must be on our guard against the enemy hidden within. Our best way of overcoming this inner enemy is to love the one who is attacking us from without.

The unique and supreme proof of love is this: to love a person who opposes us. That is why Truth himself bore the suffering of the cross, and even be-stowed his love on his persecutors. He said, *Father, forgive them, for they know not what they do.*

Should we marvel that his living disciples love their enemies when their dying Master loved his? He expressed the extent of his love when he said that *no one has greater love than this, to lay down his life for his friends.* The Lord had come to die even for his enemies. He said that he would *lay down his life for his friends* to show us that when we are able to win over our enemies by our love for them, then even our persecutors are our friends.

But no one is persecuting us to the point of death, and so how can we prove that we love our friends? In fact there is something we ought to do during times of peace to make clear whether we are strong enough to die for the sake of love during a time of persecution. John, the author of the gospel I have been quoting from, says in his first letter: *Those who have this world's goods and see a brother or sister in need, and who close their hearts, how does God's love dwell in them?* And John the Baptist says: *Let one who has two coats give to one who has none.* Will those who refuse to give up a coat for the sake of God during a time of peace give up their lives during a persecution? You must cultivate the virtue of love during times of tranquility by showing mercy, and then your love will be unconquerable in a time of chaos. First you must learn to give up your possessions for almighty God, and then yourself.

You are my friends.... How great is our Creator's mercy! We were unworthy servants, and he calls us friends! How great is our human dignity, that we should be friends of God! Now listen to what this dignity costs: *if you do what I command you*. And we have already heard that *this is my commandment, that you love one another*.

15 + PATIENCE

By your patience will you gain possession of your lives. Patience is the root and guardian of all the virtues. We gain possession of our lives by patience, since when we learn to govern ourselves, we begin to gain possession of the very thing we are.

True patience consists in bearing calmly the evils others do to us, and in not being consumed by resentment against those who inflict them. Those who only appear to bear the evils done them by their neighbors, who suffer them in silence while they are looking for an opportunity for revenge, are not practicing patience, but only making a show of it. Paul writes that *love is patient and kind*. It is patient in bearing the evils done to us by others, and it is kind in even loving those it bears with. Jesus himself tells us: *Love your enemies, do good to those who hate you, pray for those who persecute and calumniate you*. Virtue in the sight of others is to bear with those who oppose us, but virtue in God's sight is to love them. This is the only sacrifice acceptable to God.

But often we appear to be patient only because we are unable to repay the evils we suffer from others. As

I have said, those who don't pay back evil only because they can't are not patient. We are not looking to have patience on the surface, but in the heart.

The vice of impatience destroys teaching, and teaching is the nurse of the virtues. It is written that *your teaching is known by your patience.* The less people have been taught, the less patient they prove to be. No one can teach goodness to others without knowing how to endure calmly the evils done by others. It is Solomon again who discloses how high patience is on the scale of the virtues: *Better to be patient than to be brave, a master of yourself than one who takes cities.* Taking cities is a lesser victory because what we conquer then is outside of ourselves; a greater victory is won by patience when it enables people to bear with others, because then they have triumphed over themselves.

But be aware that often at the time when patient people are suffering opposition or bearing insults they feel no distress; at that time they exercise patience and maintain their innocence of heart. After a while, though, they may call to mind the things they have endured, and flare up with violent resentment. Then they seek ways of getting revenge, and they lose their earlier gentleness. Thus they pass judgment on themselves by their change of heart.

The devil, our cunning opponent, stirs up war against two persons. One he rouses to be the first to inflict an injury, and he provokes the one who has been harmed to reprisals. He is already the victor over the person he stirred up to commit the injury, and if he can't stir up the other to return it, his resentment is fierce. Thus it happens that the devil rises up with all his strength against the one he sees has borne the injury bravely. Since he couldn't rouse this one when the injury occurred, he withdraws for a time from the open contest. He looks for a chance to deceive the sufferer's heart. Though he has lost in open battle, he is still on fire to exercise his treacherous arts. In a period of tranquility he returns to the patient one's mind, and recalls the losses and injuries the sufferer has put up with. He greatly exaggerates everything that was done, shows that it was intolerable, and stirs up a peaceful heart to such a pitch of fury that often it is taken captive even after first experiencing the triumph of patience. Now ashamed at having borne the injuries calmly, and regretting that they were not revenged, the one who first suffered in patience seeks to do worse to the other if an opportunity occurs.

Who can we say this man or woman resembles except those who are victorious on the field of battle, but later through their carelessness are captured within the confines of the city? Whom do they resemble but those attacked by serious illness, who survive it only to die of a slight recurring fever? Those who truly live patiently bear with the evil done them by others: they don't resent it at the time, and they rejoice when they think back over it, glad that they endured it. They don't want to have the good of patience, which they kept safe when they were greatly disturbed, perish during a period of calm.

16 + DOUBT

Now Thomas, one of the twelve, who was called the Twin, was not with them when Jesus came. This one disciple was absent. When he returned and heard what had happened, he refused to believe what he heard. The Lord came again, and offered his side for the unbelieving disciple to touch. He showed his hands; and by showing the traces of his own wounds he healed Thomas's wound of unbelief.

What, my friends, do you learn from this? Do you think that it was by chance that this chosen disciple was absent? And that on coming later he heard what had happened, and that when he heard he doubted, and that in his doubting he touched Jesus, and that when he touched him he believed? This did not happen by chance, but by God's providence. Divine compassion brought it about in a wonderful way, so that when the doubting disciple touched the wounds in his Master's flesh he healed the wounds of our unbelief as well as his own. Thomas's unbelief was of more advantage to our faith than was the belief of the other disciples. When he was led to faith by touching Jesus, our hearts were relieved of all doubt and made firm in faith.

After his resurrection Jesus allowed his disciple to doubt, but he did not desert him in his doubt. It is much the same as when before his birth he desired that Mary have a husband, one who had not yet married her. The disciple who doubted and touched became a witness to the truth of the resurrection in much the same way as the husband of his mother had been the guardian of her perfect virginity.

Thomas touched him and cried out: *My Lord and my God. Jesus said to him: Because you have seen me, you have believed.* When Scripture says that *faith is the ground of things to be hoped for, the proof of things that are not evident,* it makes clear that faith is the proof of those things which cannot be made evident: things that are evident no longer involve faith, but knowledge. Why, when Thomas saw and touched him, did Jesus say, *Because you have seen me, you have believed?* Thomas saw one thing, and he believed another. No mortal could see his divine nature. Thomas saw a human being, and he confessed that he was God, saying *My Lord and my God.* Seeing, he believed. He looked upon a man, and testified that he was the invisible God.

Let us rejoice at what follows! *Blessed are they who have not seen and have believed.* Certainly this refers to us. We hold in our hearts one whom we do not see in his body. He refers to us, but only if we follow up our faith with our works. Those people truly believe who express their belief through their works.

17 + BELIEF

That the Lord's disciples were slow to believe in his resurrection was not so much a result of their want of strength as it was our future strength, if I may put it that way. In their state of doubt, Jesus showed them many proofs of his resurrection. What happens to us when we read and accept them is that we are strengthened as a result of their doubt. Mary Magdalene, who was quick to believe, has helped me less than Thomas, who remained so long in doubt. Thomas, doubting, touched the Lord's wounds, and healed the wound of doubt in our hearts.

Let us see what Luke reports, in order to teach us the truth of the Lord's resurrection. *While Jesus was eating, he told them not to depart from Jerusalem*; and a little farther, *As they were looking on he was lifted up, and a cloud took him from their sight*. Take note of the words he uses, and acknowledge the mysteries they express. *While he was eating...he was lifted up*. He ate, and he ascended. His was a real body: we know because he ate.

Mark recalls that before he ascended into heaven the Lord rebuked his disciples for their hardness of heart and their lack of belief. He told them that *one who believes and is baptized will be saved; one who does not believe will be condemned*. We may all be saying to ourselves, "I have believed, I will be saved." What we are saying is true—if we express our faith in our actions. True faith does not contradict its words by its conduct. That is why Paul said of certain false believers: *They profess that they know God, but they deny him by their deeds*; and why John said that *He who says that he knows God and does not observe his commandments is a liar*.

Since this is so, we must confess the reality of our faith by expressing it in our lives. Then are we true believers when we fulfill by our works what we promise by our words. On our baptismal day we promised to renounce all the works of the devil, our ancient enemy, and all his delights. We must all of us recall this before our minds. If you are sure that you are preserving after baptism what you promised before it, you can rejoice that you are believers!

But you know that you have not preserved what you promised, that you have fallen into doing what you shouldn't do, and to desiring the delights of the world. Let us see now if you can be sorry for your misdeeds. Our merciful Judge will not hold you dishonest if you return to the truth even after you have lied about your belief. In his judgment our all-powerful God puts away our misdeeds as he gladly accepts our repentance.

18 ✦ COMPASSION

In a monastery in the territory of Lycaonia there was a monk of very holy life named Martyrius. One day he was making his way from his own monastery to another, in order to visit the spiritual father there. As he was proceeding along the road he came upon a leper, whose limbs were covered with the sores caused by elephantiasis. The leper said that he wanted to return to the place he was staying, but was too exhausted to do so. He indicated that this place was on the road along which Martyrius was hurrying. The man of God pitied the leper's exhaustion, and immediately spread out the cloak he was wearing on the ground. He laid the leper on the cloak and wrapped him in it, raised him upon his shoulders, and bore him along with him.

As Martyrius was approaching the monastery gates, the spiritual father of the monastery began to cry out in a loud voice: "Hurry, open the monastery gates quickly! Brother Martyrius is coming, carrying the Lord!" As soon as Martyrius reached the gates, the one he thought was a leper leapt down from his shoulders and revealed himself as Jesus. As Martyrius looked on, he returned to heaven and said as he was ascending: "Martyrius, you did not feel shame for me upon earth. I will not feel shame for you in heaven."

As soon as the holy man entered the monastery, the abbot said to him, "Martyrius, where is the one you were carrying?" Martyrius answered him, "If I had known who he was, I would have held on to his feet." Then he said that when he was carrying him he had not felt any weight at all. Are you surprised at this? How could he feel the weight of one who was bearing his bearer?

What we must consider in this story is the great value of compassion, and how closely a merciful heart unites us to almighty God. We draw near to the One who is above all things by lowering ourselves through compassion for our neighbor. In physical things we reach the heights by stretching upward; in spiritual matters we can be certain that the further compassion draws us downward, the more surely do we approach the heights. It was not enough for the Redeemer of the human race to reveal that he would say at the final judgment, *Whenever you did it to one of the least of these my brothers and sisters, you did it to me.* It was also necessary for him to show this beforehand in himself. He wanted to show us that all those who now do good to the needy are doing it for the sake of the One whose love makes them do it. And the less contempt they have for any person who appears to be contemptible, the greater will be their recompense.

What body from among all human bodies is more sublime than Christ's, which was raised above the angels? What human body is more repulsive than a leper's, with its open and stinking wounds? Christ appeared in the likeness of a leper; Christ, whom we must revere above all, did not disdain to have us despise him as beneath all. Why did he do this? Was it not to counsel us, who are slow to learn, that anyone eager to be with him in heaven should not refuse to become humble on earth, that we should not refuse to be compassionate even toward repulsive and contemptible brothers and sisters?

I was intending to speak briefly, but because *the way of a man is not in himself* my sermon has run on and I haven't been able to restrain it. The One of whom I speak determines it, he who lives and reigns with the Father in the unity of the Holy Spirit, God for ever and ever.

19 ✦ RIGHTEOUSNESS

Summer is hard for me physically, and has brought about a long interruption in my explanations of the gospel. But because I've been silent my love has not ceased. I'm only saying what you all know within yourselves. Our expression of love is often hindered by other concerns; it remains undiminished in our hearts even though our actions do not show it. When the sun is covered with clouds we on earth can't see it, but it is still there in the sky. It is the same with love: it produces energy within us even if it does not reveal itself outwardly in our activities. But it is time now for me to speak again. Your enthusiasm is stirring me as I see you eagerly awaiting my words.

You've heard in the gospel, my friends, that sinners and tax collectors drew near our Redeemer, and that he received them. Not only did he talk with them, he even took meals with them. When the Pharisees saw this, they felt scorn for him. From this you should conclude that true righteousness has compassion, but false righteousness scorn—though even the righteous are apt to be justly indignant with sinners.

What is done as a result of pride is one thing, and what is done out of zeal for discipline is another. The righteous show scorn without being scornful; they despair without despairing; when they stir up hostility they do it out of love. Even though outwardly they heap up reproofs for the sake of discipline, inwardly their love causes them to remain kind. Often in their own hearts they put those they are correcting ahead of themselves, and consider those they are judging better than themselves. In doing this the discipline they exercise shows their concern for those under them, while their humility shows their concern for themselves.

On the other hand, those who are used to feeling proud because of their false righteousness look down on everyone else. They show no mercy to the weak, and the more convinced they are that they are not sinners, the worse sinners they become. The Pharisees were people of this type. They passed judgment on the Lord because he received sinners; their dried-up hearts found fault with the fountain of mercy.

20 ✛ MARTYRDOM

Today we are celebrating a martyr's birth into the life of heaven. If we are striving with the Lord's help to live out the virtue of patience, we hold the palm of martyrdom even though we are living in a time of peace. There are in fact two kinds of martyrdom. One takes place only in the heart, the other in both heart and body. We too are capable of being martyrs, even without having anyone slay us. To die from someone's enmity is martyrdom out in the open; to bear insults, to love a person who hates us, is martyrdom in secret.

Jesus testified to both of these kinds of martyrdom, one that takes place in our hearts, the other in public. He asked the sons of Zebedee, *Are you able to drink from the cup that I am to drink?* When they immediately answered, *We are able,* he replied, *You will indeed drink from my cup.* What do we take his cup to be if not his passion, of which he said elsewhere: *Father, if it be possible, let this cup pass from me?* But in fact the sons of Zebedee, James, that is, and John, did not both die as martyrs. Each heard that he would drink from the cup, but John's life did not end in public martyrdom. Even so, he was a martyr. He sustained in his heart the suffering he did not undergo in his body. We too, following his example, can be unbloody martyrs if we truly hold to patience in our hearts.

Hold to patience in your hearts, my friends, and put it into action when the situation calls for it. Don't let any abusive word from your neighbor stir up hatred in you, and don't allow any loss of things that pass away to upset you. If you are steadfast in fearing the loss of those things that last forever, you will never take seriously the loss of those that pass away; if you keep your eyes fixed on the glory of our eternal recompense, you will not resent a temporal injury. You must bear with those who oppose you, but also love those you bear with. Seek an eternal reward in return for your temporal losses.

None of you should count on being able to carry this out on your own. Obtain it by your prayers, asking God who commands to provide it. We know that God gladly listens to those who ask him to grant what he commands. When we continually besiege him in prayer, God quickly comes to our assistance in temptation.

21 + HOSPITALITY

The gospel tells us that the Lord appeared to two disciples while they were walking on the road. Even though they did not believe in him, they were talking about him. He did not appear to them in a form they could recognize: as he was to the eyes of their hearts, a stranger, so was he to their bodily eyes. Inwardly they were full of love and of doubt. The Lord was outwardly present to them, but he did not reveal to them who he was. He showed himself to them as they were talking about him, but because of their doubts he hid the appearance that would allow them to recognize him.

As they walked along, he did indeed talk with them, reproving the hardness of their understanding, and opening to them the mysteries of the Scriptures concerning himself. Yet, because as an object of faith he was still a stranger to their hearts, he made a pretence of going on farther. Truth was not acting deceitfully here. He was only showing himself to them in accordance with their thoughts about him. They had to be tested as to whether those who did not as yet love him as God were at least able to love him as a stranger.

Because those with whom Truth was walking couldn't be completely alien to love, they invited him, a stranger, to be their guest. They set the table, brought food, and in the breaking of bread they recognized the God they did not know when he was explaining the Scriptures to them. They were not enlightened by hearing God's commandments, but by their own actions, for it is written: *It is not hearers of the law who are righteous before God, but doers of the law will be made righteous.* Let those who want to understand what they have heard be quick to fulfill in action what they have already been able to understand. The disciples did not recognize their Lord when he was speaking; the Lord allowed himself to be recognized as he was being fed.

My friends, love hospitality, love the works of mercy. Paul said: *Let the love of the brotherhood remain, and do not forget hospitality; it was by this that some have*

been *made acceptable, having entertained angels hospi-
tably*; and Peter told us to be *hospitable to one another,
without complaint*; and Truth himself said: *I needed
hospitality, and you welcomed me.* And yet often we
feel no inclination to offer the gift of hospitality. But
consider, my friends, how great this virtue of hospitality is! Receive Christ at your tables, so that he will receive you at the eternal banquet. Offer hospitality
now to Christ the stranger, so that at the judgment
you will not be a stranger but he will accept you into
his kingdom as one he knows.

22 ✦ GOOD WILL

The kingdom of God has no assessed value. It is
worth everything you have. To Zacchaeus it was
worth half his possessions; the other half he kept back
in order to restore fourfold anything that he had un-
justly taken. To Peter and Andrew it was worth their
nets and boat. To the widow it was worth two small
coins. To someone else it is worth a cup of cold
water. As I said, the kingdom of God is worth everything you have. Think about it, my friends. There's
nothing cheaper when you go to buy it, and nothing
more valuable once you have it.

But suppose you don't even have a cup of cold
water to offer to someone who needs it. Even then
God's Word reassures us. When our Redeemer was
born heavenly voices cried out, *Glory to God in the
highest, and peace on earth to people of good will!* In

God's sight no hand is ever empty of a gift if the heart is filled with good will. The Psalmist says, *The offerings of praise I will make to you, O God, are in me.* He means that although you may have no outward gift to offer, you can find within yourself something to place on the altar of God's praise. God has no need of anything we can give, and is better pleased with the offering of our hearts.

There is nothing we can offer to God more precious than good will. But what is good will? To have good will is to experience concern for someone else's adversities as if they were our own; to give thanks for our neighbor's prosperity as for our own; to believe that another person's loss is our own, and also that another's gain is ours; to love a friend in God, and bear with an enemy out of love; to do to no one what we do not want to suffer ourselves, and to refuse to no one what we rightly want for ourselves; to choose to help a neighbor who is in need not only to the whole extent of our ability, but even beyond our means. What offering is richer, what offering is more substantial than this one? What we are offering to God on the altar of our hearts is the sacrifice of ourselves!

But we never fully accomplish this offering of our good will unless we leave completely behind our craving for the things of this world. If we crave anything in the world then surely we envy our neighbors who possess it. Doesn't it always seem that we are lacking what someone else has gained? Envy is so much opposed to good will that once it invades our hearts, good will disappears. Holy people, who want to be able to love their neighbors completely, have always striven to love nothing in this world, to seek nothing, to possess and even to desire nothing.

23 ✦ PRAYING FOR OUR ENEMIES

When our hearts are reluctant we often have to compel ourselves to pray for our enemies, to pour out prayer for those who are against us. Would that our hearts were filled with love! How frequently we offer a prayer for our enemies, but do it because we are commanded to, not out of love for them. We ask the gift of life for them even while we are afraid that our prayer may be heard. The Judge of our souls considers our hearts rather than our words. Those who do not pray for their enemies out of love are not asking anything for their benefit.

But suppose they have committed a serious offense against us? Suppose they have inflicted losses on those who support them, and have injured them? Suppose they have persecuted their friends? We might legitimately keep these things in mind if we had no offenses of our own to be forgiven.

Jesus, who is our advocate, has composed a prayer for our case and in this case the one who pleads our case is also our judge. There is a condition he has inserted in the prayer he composed which reads: *Forgive us our debts, as we also forgive our debtors.* Since our advocate is the one coming to be our judge, he is listening to the prayer he himself composed for our use. Perhaps we say the words, *Forgive us our debts, as we also forgive our debtors*, without carrying them out, and thus our words bind us more tightly; or perhaps we omit this condition in our prayer, and then our advocate does not recognize the prayer which he composed for us, and says to himself: "I know what I taught them. This is not the prayer I gave them."

What are we to do then, my friends? We are to bestow our love on our brothers and sisters. We must not allow any malice at all to remain in our hearts. May almighty God have regard for our love of our neighbor, so that he may pardon our iniquities! Remember what he has taught us: *Forgive, and you will be forgiven*. People are in debt to us, and we to them. Let us forgive them their debts, so that what we owe may be forgiven us. But our hearts struggle against this. They want to do what they have been told, but there is something that makes them reluctant to do so.

We are gathered at a martyr's tomb. We know by what kind of death this martyr reached the kingdom of heaven. If we do not lay down our lives for Christ, let us at least conquer our hearts. God is appeased by this sacrifice. At the time of his loving judgment he will approve the victory which is our peace. He sees the struggle going on in our hearts, and he helps those who struggle, just as he will later reward those who conquer.

24 ✦ THE POOR

Reflect on the story of Lazarus and the rich man, my friends, and behave shrewdly. Seek intercessors for your sins. Look to the poor to be your advocates on the day of judgment.

At the present time you have many Lazaruses. They are lying outside your houses and your places of business; they are in continual need of what falls from your table after you have been satisfied. The words of the gospel instruct us how to fulfill Christ's precepts. Everyday, if we look for Lazarus, we find him; every day, even if we don't look for him, we see him. The poor persist in being present. Those who beg from us may later come forward to intercede for us. We are the ones who ought to be begging, and yet they beg from us! Consider whether we should deny what they ask from us, when it is our benefactors who are asking! Do not squander this time of mercy, do not waste the gifts you yourselves have received.

Think about suffering before it comes to you. When you see the wretched of this world, even if what they are doing seems blameworthy, you must not look down on them. Perhaps the medicine of poverty will heal those who are wounded by some weakness in their character.

If you see faults to criticize in them, you can turn this to your advantage; their vices can bring about an increase of holiness in you. When you give bread together with a word, the bread of restoration with a word of counsel, the person who asked one kind of sustenance from you receives two. His physical self is satisfied with food, and his inner self with a message.

Therefore when we see poor persons who need guidance we are to counsel them and not despise them. If there is nothing in them to reprove, we must honor them as our intercessors. But we see many people of whose strengths we are unaware. Therefore we must honor them all: you must humble yourselves before everyone, inasmuch as you do not know who among them may be Christ.

My friends, you must learn to despise all passing things, you must learn to reject short-lived honors and to love eternal glory. You must honor the poor. Consider that those you see experiencing the world's contempt are within themselves friends of God. Share your possessions with them, so that in the end they may deign to share what they have with you. Reflect on what the teacher of the Gentiles says: *Let your abundance at the present time supply their want, so that their abundance may supply your want.* Reflect on what Jesus himself said: *As you did it for one of the least of these my brothers and sisters, you did it for me.* Why do you hesitate to make a gift? What you reach out to offer to a person lying prostrate on the ground you are

giving to One who is seated in heaven. May almighty
God, who is addressing these things to your ears
through me, himself address them to your hearts!

DISCIPLESHIP

FROM NOW ON YOU WILL
BE CATCHING MEN
LK 5·10

J esus said to them: Peace be with you. As the Father sent me, I also send you. The Father sent his son, appointing him to become flesh for the redemption of the human race. He willed him to come into the world to suffer—and yet he loved this Son he sent to suffer. In this passage of the holy gospel the Lord is sending his chosen apostles into the world, not to enjoy it, but to suffer in it, just as he himself was sent. Therefore as the Son is loved by the Father and yet is sent to suffer, so also the disciples are loved by the Lord, even though he sends them too into the world to suffer. When he says, As the Father sent me, I also send you, he means, "When I send you out amid the hardships your persecutors will bring upon you, I am loving you with that love with which the Father loved me when he sent me into the world to suffer."

We can also interpret this "sending" in terms of his divine nature. The Son is said to be sent from the Father from the fact that he is begotten by the Father. The Son relates that he sends the Holy Spirit, which, though coequal with the Father and the Son, yet did not become flesh. He says: When the Paraclete comes, whom I am sending to you from the Father. If being sent could be understood only in the sense of becoming flesh, the Holy Spirit could in no way be called "sent" since the Spirit did not become flesh. The sending of the Spirit is that procession by which the Spirit proceeds from the Father and the Son. So, as the Spirit is said to be sent because proceeding, so too the Son is sent because begotten.

26 + SELF-RENUNCIATION

Our Lord and Redeemer entered the world as a new kind of human being and gave the world new teachings. He offered the contrast of his new way of life to our old one, which was nurtured by our vices. What did our old and carnal nature know how to do except to hang on to its own belongings, to seize if it could what belonged to someone else, and to covet what it could not seize?

Our Physician brought from heaven remedies for every single moral fault. The medical art cures fevers with cold compresses, and chills by applying heat. Similarly Jesus prescribed qualities contrary to our sins: self-restraint to the undisciplined, generosity to the stingy, gentleness to the irritable, and humility to the proud. When he announced these new teachings to his followers, he told them that *whoever of you do not renounce all that you have cannot be my disciple*. He means that you who are coveting what belongs to someone else out of your old way of life are to be generous even with what belongs to you out of zeal for the new way.

But let us listen to Christ's words: *Those who would come after me must renounce themselves*. He tells us that we must renounce ourselves. Some may not find it difficult to abandon their possessions, but it is extremely difficult for us to abandon ourselves. Renouncing what we have is not so much; renouncing what we are amounts to a great deal.

The Lord tells us who are coming to him to renounce ourselves because, as we are coming to the public test of our faith, we are taking up the struggle against evil spirits. Evil spirits possess nothing of their own in this world. We must be naked if we are to struggle with other naked beings. If those who are clothed begin to struggle with others who are naked they are quickly thrown to the ground, since they offer something to grasp. What are earthly things except a kind of covering for our bodies? Let us who are preparing for a contest with the devil cast off this clothing so that we won't be overcome. Let us hold no possessions in this world through our love for them; we shouldn't seek to take pleasure in things that are passing away lest the devil grab hold of the desires which clothe us and bring us down.

But abandoning our possessions isn't enough if we do not abandon ourselves as well. What can "abandoning ourselves" mean? If we abandon ourselves, where are we to go outside of ourselves? And who is it who goes, if we forsake ourselves?

We are one thing in the nature with which we were created, and another when we have fallen into sin; what we have done is one thing, what we have become is another. Let us abandon the selves we have become by sinning, and let us continue to be the selves we have become by grace. Think of those who were proud—if they have turned to Christ and become humble they have abandoned themselves; those of unrestrained desires, who have changed to a life of self-restraint, have certainly denied what they were. Misers, those who used to seize what belongs to others, but who have stopped trying to get ahead and learned to be generous with what belongs to themselves, have beyond all doubt abandoned themselves. They are now the persons they were created to be. It is written, *Change the wicked, and they will be no more.* The wicked who have changed will be no more, not because they will altogether cease to exist in their essential being, but because they will cease to exist in their sinful state.

We abandon ourselves, we renounce ourselves, when we escape from what we were in our old state, and strive toward what we are called to be in our new one. Let us see how Paul, who said *It is no longer I who live,* renounced himself: the cruel persecutor was destroyed and the holy preacher began to live. But how was Paul, who said that he was no longer living, able to proclaim the message of truth? Immediately after saying *It is no longer I who live,* he added, *but Christ lives in me.* He means that he had indeed been destroyed by himself, since he no longer lived unspiritually, but in his essential being he was not dead since he was spiritually alive in Christ.

Paul is saying just what Christ said: *Those who would come after me must renounce themselves.* We cannot go beyond ourselves if we do not know how to sacrifice ourselves. We transplant seedlings to help them grow, and so we can say that we uproot them in order to make them increase. Seeds disappear when we put them in the earth, and then spring up to renew their kind; it seems as if what they were is being lost, but that is how they receive the ability to become what they were not.

But those who have renounced their vices still have to seek the virtues that will make them grow. After saying that *those who would come after me must deny themselves,* the Lord immediately adds that *they must take up their cross daily and follow him.* There are two ways we can take up our cross: we can affect our bodies through abstinence, and we can afflict our hearts through compassion for our neighbor. Paul took up his cross in both ways. He said, *I discipline my body and subdue it, lest after preaching to others I myself should be rejected.* That is the physical cross which affected his body. He also took up the interior cross of compassion for his neighbor: *Who is weak, and I am not weak? Who is caused to fall, and I am not aflame with indignation?* As an example to us he carried the cross of abstinence in his body; and since he took on himself the harm caused by someone else's weakness, he carried a cross in his heart.

27 + RICHES

Some people consider that the commandments of the Old Testament are stricter than those of the New, but their interpretation is short-sighted and they are deceived. In the Old Testament theft is punished, but not miserliness. A wrongful taking of property was punished by a fourfold restitution. The rich man in the gospel, however, was not admonished for having taken away someone else's property, but punished for not giving away his own. It is not said that he forcibly wronged anyone, but that he prided himself on what he had received from God as a gift.

It is principally from this parable of the rich man and Lazarus that we can infer what punishment those people will receive who plunder the property of others, if those who do not give of their own are punished in hell. We should not judge ourselves safe, saying, "See, I never seize the property of another person, but I enjoy what is lawfully mine." The rich man was not punished for taking away anyone else's property, but for falling prey to evil after acquiring possessions of his own. This was why he was handed over to be tormented in hell. He was perfectly contented; he used the gifts he received for building up his feelings of superiority; he had no knowledge of the essentials of kindness; and he refused to make reparation for his sins, even when the opportunity was available to him.

28   +   THE DANGER OF RICHES

We must ponder the answer Abraham gave to the rich man in the gospel when he asked to be given a drop of water from Lazarus' finger. *Son, remember that you received good things in your lifetime, and Lazarus in like manner evil things; now he is being comforted here, while you are in anguish.* That sentence, my friends, clearly demands an anxious hearing more than an explanation. If any of you have received some material goods in this world, you ought to be very much frightened of them, if I may say so. Perhaps they were given you in return for some good you did, in which case the Judge who is paying you in this life with external goods may deprive you of interior ones; the honors and riches you receive here may be for you not an aid to virtue, but your payment for the work you've done.

The words *You received good things in your lifetime* indicate that the rich man had done something good for which he received good things in this life. Again, when Lazarus is said to have received *evil things*, we are shown that there was some evil that was to be cleansed away. The fire of poverty cleansed Lazarus of his evil deeds, and happiness in this passing life rewarded the rich man's good deeds. Poverty afflicted the former and cleansed him; wealth rewarded the latter, and deprived him of everything else.

I am speaking to you who are well off in this world: whenever you remember that you have received good things for the good you do, be afraid lest this prosperity which has been granted you may be your only reward. Whenever you see the poor continually doing things that are wrong, do not despise them or despair of them; poverty may be cleansing them of the superficial stains produced by their wickedness. You must be anxious for yourselves, since you know that a prosperous life may follow evil actions. You must be solicitous for the poor, because poverty is their teacher, afflicting them until it leads them to righteousness.

29 + TRUE RICHES

Jesus told the crowd, *A sower went out to sow his seed. And, as he sowed, some fell along the path and was trampled on, and the birds of the air devoured it. And some fell on rock, and as it came up it withered because it had no moisture. And some fell among thorns, and the thorns grew with it and choked it. And some fell on good ground, and grew and produced its crop a hundredfold.*

If I were to tell you that the seed in the Lord's parable of the sower denotes the word, the field the world, the birds demons, and the thorns riches, you might be reluctant to believe me. And so the Lord himself explained what he was saying, to make it clear that he was speaking figuratively, and so that you could be certain of the meaning I am struggling to explain.

Who would believe me if I chose to interpret the thorns as riches, particularly as thorns pierce us and riches delight us? And yet riches are thorns. They wound our hearts by piercing them with thoughts of themselves, and they bloody our hearts by enticing them to sin. The evangelist is our witness that in another place the Lord called them not simply riches, but *deceitful riches*. And they are deceitful, in that they cannot remain with us long; they are deceitful in that they do not relieve the poverty of our hearts. The only true riches are the ones that make us rich in virtues. Therefore, my friends, if you want to be rich you must love true riches. If you seek genuine honors, reach out for the heavenly kingdom. If you love the glories of rank, hasten to be enrolled in the court of the angels on high.

30 ✛ LOVE AND HATE

When we reflect on what is promised us in heaven, everything we have on earth comes to appear worthless. When we compare our earthly possessions with the happiness of heaven, they seem a burden and not a help. When we compare our life in time with eternal life, we have to call it death rather than life. What is our daily decline into decomposition and decay but a kind of extension of death? Who can describe the joys of heaven? Whose mind can grasp them? There we will take part with the choirs of angels, we will share with the blessed spirits in our

Creator's glory, we will see the face of God before us and behold infinite light, we will feel no fear of death but rejoice in the gift of everlasting life!

Even to hear these things sets us on fire! We are filled with longing to be where we hope to rejoice without end. But great rewards come only through great labors. Paul teaches that *no one is crowned who does not compete according to the rules*. The great reward delights us; we must not be discouraged by the laborious struggle that precedes it. Jesus says to those coming to him: *If anyone comes to me and does not hate his father and mother and wife and children and brothers and sisters, and even his own life, he cannot be my disciple.*

We must carefully inquire how he can command us to hate our parents and relatives when he has ordered us to love even our enemies. He himself says of married couples, *What God has joined together, let no one separate*; and Paul says, *Husbands, love your wives, as Christ loved the Church*. The disciple preaches that we must love our wives even though his Master says that a person who *does not hate his wife cannot be my disciple*. Does a judge announce one thing and the herald proclaim another? Or can we hate and love at the same time?

If we study our Lord's precept we find that we are capable of both hating and loving, but we have to make a distinction. We must love those who are united to us by some natural relationship in that they are our neighbors, and we must hate them and avoid them insofar as they hold us back on our way to God. We can say that we love those who are wise in the world's ways by hating them when we refuse to listen to the evil things they suggest to us.

And the Lord, to show us that this hatred directed toward our neighbors does not arise from lack of feeling, but from love, added immediately that such a one *hates even his own life.* He has instructed us to hate our neighbors, and our own lives as well. Those who hate their neighbors as themselves are to hate them by loving them. We hate our own life in the right way when we do not give in to its physical desires, when we restrain its appetites, when we resist its desire for pleasure. If we despise our own life, and lead it to a better state, we are, as it were, loving it by hating it. But we must surely make a distinction in hating our neighbors: we must love in them what they are, and hate in them anything that causes them to hinder us in our journey toward God.

When Paul was on his way toward Jerusalem, the prophet Agabus took his belt and bound his own feet with it, saying: *So will they bind at Jerusalem the man whose belt this is.* What did Paul say, this man who hated his own life perfectly? *I am ready not only to be bound but even to die at Jerusalem for the name of the Lord Jesus Christ. I put no value on my life.* See how he loved his life by hating it! In hating his life he was loving what he longed to deliver up to death for

Jesus, so that Jesus might raise it to life from the death of sin.

Let us draw from this distinction between the kinds of hatred an understanding of what we are to feel toward our neighbors. Let us love all those who are in any way opposed to us, but let us not love someone who is an obstacle along our road to God, even someone related to us. All those eagerly longing for the things of eternity must, in the cause of God they are undertaking, move beyond father, mother, wife, children, relatives; they must move beyond themselves, that they may get to know God more truly. Unspiritual feelings divide the heart and obscure its vision, but they do not harm us if we hold them in check. We are, then, to love our neighbors; we are to offer our love to all, relatives and strangers alike, without being turned aside from the love of God.

31 ✛ GIVE FREELY

Jesus gave his disciples the power to preach, and to perform miracles. Let us now learn what else he taught them: *You received freely, give freely.* He foresaw that there would be some who would turn the gift of the Spirit they had received to business use, who would yield to the sin of avarice by debasing the miracles they were performing. Thus Simon the magician, seeing miracles worked by the laying on of hands, wanted to pay for the gift of the Holy Spirit.

He would then be able to commit a greater sin by selling what he had improperly purchased.[†]

Thus too our Redeemer made a scourge of cords and drove the crowds out of the temple, overturning the seats of those who were selling doves.

Selling doves means granting the laying on of hands, by which the Spirit is conveyed, not for the worthiness of the recipient's life but for a price. Some indeed are not paid in money for an ordination; they bestow holy orders to win human favor, and the recompense they are looking for is people's esteem. Surely these are not giving freely what they have received freely, because they are seeking to be paid in acclaim for the holy office they have conferred. The prophet Isaiah, when he was describing the righteous, said that *they keep their hands clean of every gift.* He specified *every gift* because gifts come by many ways— by deference, by hand, by mouth. The gift we give by deference is submission when submission is undeserved; the gift we hand out is money; the gift of our mouths is acclaim. Those who bestow holy orders *keep their hands clean of every gift* when they demand not only no money but not even human favor for the sacred gifts.

[†] See the Acts of the Apostles, 8.9-24. Gregory is speaking of simony, the buying and selling of sacred actions or things, which takes its name from this Simon.

My friends who are involved in secular matters, you are familiar with my affairs. Turn your attention to your own. Do everything you do for one another freely. Don't seek repayment for your work in this world. As you want to hide your bad actions so that no one will see them, so take care that your good deeds don't come to light and earn you the esteem of others. Don't do any evil, and don't do good for the sake of a passing reward. Seek to have as the only witness of your work the Judge whose judgment you await. Let him see the good you do in secret, so that he can reveal it to everyone on the day when he grants you your reward.

Every day you provide your bodies with food to keep them from failing. In the same way your good works should be the daily nourishment of your hearts. Your bodies are fed with food and your spirits with good works. You aren't to deny your soul, which is going to live forever, what you grant to your body, which is going to die.

If your house should suddenly catch fire you would seize what you value and run. You would count as gain whatever you took with you out of the flames. You can see that a fire of calamities is burning up the world, laying waste everything you thought beautiful. Count yourself well off if you carry anything out of the world, if you take anything with you as you flee, if you preserve by giving it away what would have perished had it remained yours. We lose all our earthly possessions if we save them, but by bestowing them on others we save them. Time is running out. We are being hurried irresistibly into the presence of our Judge: let us be eager to prepare ourselves for him by our good deeds.

32 ✛ A PROPHET'S REWARD

Jesus said that *those who receive a prophet because he or she bears the name of prophet will have a prophet's reward, and those who receive a just person because he or she is just will have a just person's reward.* We must note that he did not say that they will get a reward from the prophet, or from the just person, but that they *will have a prophet's reward,* and that they *will have a just person's reward.*

What does it mean to say that a person *will have a prophet's reward?* It means that the Lord will give the reward due the gift of prophecy to those who support a prophet out of their own generosity, even though they themselves do not have the gift; and it is the same with the gift of justice. It may be that the just will have greater confidence in speaking out if they have no possessions in this world. When people who do possess something, and perhaps are not bold enough to speak out freely on behalf of justice, support those who have nothing, they make themselves sharers in their freedom. Then they may receive the reward of justice equally with those who were enabled through their support to speak their message of justice

freely. People may be filled with the spirit of prophecy, but lack food for their bodies. If they are not fed,
we can be sure that they will no longer be heard.
Those who give food to prophets because they are
prophets give them the strength to make their
prophecies, and will have a prophet's reward. They
themselves are not filled with the spirit of prophecy,
yet in God's sight they provide the means which help
the prophets to carry out their role.

Saint John wrote of some of the brothers who
were on a journey that *they have set out for the sake of
Christ's name, accepting nothing from the Gentiles. We
must support such people, that we may be fellow-workers
in the truth.* People who give material aid to those
with spiritual gifts are fellow-workers in those spiritual gifts. Not many receive spiritual gifts; many
more are rich in worldly goods. The wealthy share the
virtues of the poor when they provide relief for them
from their riches.

Through Isaiah the Lord promised spiritual virtues
to his forsaken people, that is to his church, under
the images of the trees they were longing to see in
their exile. He said: *I will make the desert a pool of
water, and trackless land into streams of water; I will put
in the wilderness the cedar and the thorn, the myrtle and
the olive; I will set in the desert the fir, the elm and the
box. Then people may see and know, and consider and
understand together.*

The Lord did indeed make the desert into a pool of water and trackless land into streams of water. He gave the flowing waters of his teaching to the Gentiles. Earlier, because of their dryness, they had been fruitless, without good works; and the way which was once closed to his teachers because of its roughness and dryness later flowed with their teaching as with brooks filled with water.

And in his generosity God promises still more: *I will put in the wilderness the cedar and the thorn.* The cedar, owing to its strong aroma and indestructible nature, we may take to refer to the promise. It points to those whose actions manifest virtues and serve as signs, those who can say with Paul, *we are the aroma of Christ to God.* Their hearts are so firmly grounded in the everlasting love that earthly love leaves them uncorrupted. Of the thorn, God said to sinful man: *Your land will bring forth thorns and nettles for you.* Does it surprise you that he promises his church the very thing he multiplied as a punishment for sinners? The thorn signifies the teachings of spiritual people. When they speak of sins and virtues, at one time they threaten eternal punishment, and at another they promise the joy of heaven. They prick their hearers' hearts and so pierce them with sorrow and compunction that tears flow from their eyes. It is as if their souls were shedding blood.

Myrtle is soothing; we use it to restore strained muscles. What does it represent, then, but people who are able to sympathize with the sufferings of their neighbors, who soothe them in their afflictions according to what Saint Paul wrote: *Thanks be to God who comforts us in all our afflictions, so that we may be able to comfort those who are in any trouble?* When they bring a good word or some help to comfort their troubled neighbors, they restore them and prevent them from falling into despair. And what are we to understand by the olive except the merciful? The harvest of mercy shines like olive oil in the sight of almighty God.

The promise continues: *I will set in the desert the fir, the elm and the box.* The fir grows tall, reaching high into the air. It designates those who though still within the church on earth are already contemplating the things of heaven. By their birth they are sprung from the earth, yet their contemplation lifts them above themselves.

And what does the elm represent but the hearts of people of the world? While they are involved in their material concerns they bear no fruit, no spiritual virtues. But although the elm has no fruit of its own, we use it to support the grapevine and its fruit. So too members of the church who lack the gifts of the spiritual virtues may provide out of their own bounty for people who are filled with spiritual gifts. When they do this it is just as if they are elm trees supporting the grapevine with its clusters of fruit.

And what does the box signify? It does not grow tall, but even though it lacks fruit it always remains green. Box signifies those who, owing to the weaknesses of age, can no longer produce good works in the church, but who still follow the beliefs of the faithful who went before them and so remain eternally green.

And then after listing the trees Isaiah says: *Then people may see and know, and consider and understand*; and with great appropriateness he adds, *together*. Since there are in our church different customs and different ministries, it is necessary that we all learn together. In the church, spiritual people with a variety of characters, ages and ministries, all have something to teach.

But you see how I have been wandering far afield over many kinds of trees while I was intending only to clarify the meaning of the elm tree. And so let me return to the place where I introduced the words of the prophet. *Those who receive a prophet because he or she bears the name of prophet will have a prophet's reward*. Even though the elm itself bears no fruit, it supports the grapevine with its fruit, and thus it accomplishes its purpose by providing well for others.

MINISTRY

I AM THE GOOD SHEPHERD * JN 10·11

Let us listen to what Christ said to the crowds about John. *What did you go out into the wilderness to see? A reed shaken by the wind?* He did not expect them to assent to this, but to deny it. As soon as a slight breeze touches a reed it bends. What then does the reed represent, if not a worldly soul? Touched by approval or malice it turns round in every direction. A slight breeze of approval comes from someone's mouth and it is cheerful and proud, bending over completely, so to speak, in the direction of being pleasant; if the breeze of praise becomes a wind of malice the reed bends quickly in the opposite direction, toward fierce anger.

John was no reed, shaken by the wind. No one's pleasant attitude made him agreeable, and no one's anger made him bitter. Prosperity could not lift him up nor adversity bring him down. He was no *reed shaken by the wind!* No change in events deflected him from his upright state. My friends, let us learn not to be reeds shaken by the wind. We must keep our minds steady before the breezes of opinion, and our hearts unbent. Malice should never provoke us to anger, nor favor make us revel in foolish enjoyment. We should not let prosperity make us proud, nor adversity trouble us. We who are firmly established in faith should not be moved at all by the vicissitudes of passing events.

The Lord continues: *But what did you go out into the wilderness to see? A man in soft garments? Behold, those who wear soft garments are in kings' houses!* John is described as wearing a garment of camel's hair, as you know. Do not think that following every changing fashion in dress is without its sins. If it were, the Lord would not have praised John for the roughness of his clothing. He said that John was not clothed in soft garments because John refused to flatter sinners with charming words. Instead, he reproved them with bitter denunciations, saying: *You brood of adders, who warned you to flee the wrath to come?* Solomon said that *the words of the wise are like goads, like nails driven deep.* The words of the wise are compared to nails and goads; instead of gently stroking the faults of evildoers, they pierce right through them.

But what did you go out into the wilderness to see? A prophet? Yes, I tell you, and more than a prophet. The ministry of a prophet is to speak of things that are going to come about, but not actually to point them out. John is more than a prophet because he pointed out the one of whom, as his forerunner, he had prophesied.

The Lord denied that John was a reed shaken by the wind, or a man clothed in soft garments, or a prophet. Let us now listen to what he could accurately say of him: *This is he of whom it is written: Behold, I am sending my angel before your face, who will prepare your way before you.*

The Greek word "angel" means "messenger." The one sent to proclaim the Judge who will come from heaven is rightly called an angel: the dignity of the name is fulfilled in the work. The name is indeed an exalted one, and John's life was not less than his name. Would that all of us who are called priests, my friends, could say without being condemned for it that we are called angels! The prophet testifies that *the lips of the priest will keep knowledge, and people will seek the law from his mouth: for he is the angel of the Lord of hosts.*

And you too, my friends, if you wish it, can be worthy of this exalted name. Each of you who can, each of you who receives the inspiration from on high to call your neighbor back from evil-doing, to encourage your neighbor to do good, to proclaim the eternal kingdom and eternal punishment to anyone astray, to communicate holy things—each one of you, when you do these things, is truly an angel.

You should never say that you are unable to give counsel, that you are not qualified to encourage anyone. Do what you can, lest you be punished for having employed badly what you received, like the man who was given only one talent, who was more eager to hide it than to use it. We know that the Lord wanted not only bowls, but also ladles in his tabernacle. The bowls signify a more than sufficient teaching, the ladles small and limited knowledge. A person full of true teaching fills his hearer's minds and so

provides a bowl by what he says; another who proclaims what she perceives as well as she can offers a
ladle full. You are in God's tabernacle, in his holy
church. If you cannot fill bowls with the wisdom of
your teaching, give your neighbors ladles filled with a
good word, as much as you have received from the divine bounty.

Be eager to have companions on your way toward
God. Any of you going to the market, or perhaps to
the public baths, will invite someone you see has
nothing else to do to come along. It is so natural we
make it a habit. So, if you are going toward God take
care not to go to him alone. It is written, *Let him who
hears say, Come!* Those how have received in their
hearts a word of heavenly love can respond with a
word of encouragement to their neighbors. They may
have no bread to give as an alms to another who is in
need, but one who has a tongue has something
greater with which to make an offering. It is worth
more to offer a nourishing word to refresh a heart that
is going to live forever than to satisfy with earthly
bread the stomach of a body that is going to die.

Do not hold back from your neighbors the alms of
a word, my friends. I am counseling myself along with
you. Keep yourselves from idle talk, and avoid useless
chatter. We must struggle against our tongues. Do not
let your words gush forth into the wind, since Christ
asks whether you do not know that on the day of
judgment you will render an account for every idle

word that proceeds from your mouth? Consider how quickly the time allotted to life runs out, and give heed to the coming of your Judge. Keep him before the eyes of your heart, and call him to your neighbors' remembrance. Then, if you do not neglect to make him known, as far as your strength allows, you may deserve to have him call you an angel along with John.

34   ✦   THE GOOD SHEPHERD

My friends, in this reading from the gospel there is instruction for you, but it also reveals a danger for me. One whose goodness is his very being and not some extraneous gift says: *I am the good shepherd.* He tells us the nature of this goodness, which he wants us to imitate, when he says: *The good shepherd lays down his life for his sheep.* He himself embodied what he taught; he was an example of what he commanded.

It is written that *all flesh is grass,* and what is grass if not nourishing vegetation? The good shepherd has laid down his life for his sheep in order to change his body and blood into a sacrament for us, to satisfy us, the sheep he has redeemed, by giving us his own flesh as food. In showing his contempt for death he shows us the way which we are to follow; he sets before us the mould which we are to conform to. We are to begin by sharing our material goods with his sheep out of compassion, and then, should it be necessary, we are to serve them even by our death.

But the hireling, who is not the shepherd, whose own the sheep are not, sees the wolf coming and leaves the sheep and flees. We can never really know whether someone is a shepherd or a hireling until they are tested. During times of peace even hirelings frequently stand up and protect the flock like true shepherds. But when the wolf comes, they then reveal what their intentions were while they were standing as protectors of the flock. Any rapacious intruder preying upon you, God's people of faith, is a wolf coming upon the sheep. Those who appeared to be shepherds, but were not, leave the sheep and flee. While they are afraid of the danger to themselves, they don't venture to resist the wrong the intruder is doing. Their flight isn't physical, but a withholding of help; it is to see the wrong the intruder is doing and to remain silent; it is to hide under the cover of silence.

Addressing people like this, the prophet said: *You have not offered any opposition, nor have you fortified the house of Israel, to hold fast in battle on the day of the Lord.* To offer opposition means to openly denounce any wrongdoing; we hold fast in battle for the house of Israel on the day of the Lord, and fortify it, if we defend innocent believers against the wrongdoing of the wicked with the authority of righteousness. Since hirelings do none of this, we can say that they flee when they see the wolf coming.

And the wolf snatches and scatters the sheep. The wolf comes, and the hireling flees. The evil spirit tears apart the hearts of believers by tempting them, and those holding the place of shepherd take no responsibility. Souls perish while they enjoy the prerogatives of their office. The wolf snatches and scatters the sheep when it carries one off in dissipation, another in greed and another in pride; it destroys one by anger, stirs up another by envy and trips up another by deceit. When the devil kills off believers through temptation, he is like a wolf dispersing the flock. No zeal rouses hirelings against these temptations, no love excites them. They seek only outward advantages, carelessly allowing internal injury to their flocks.

I am the good shepherd, Jesus said again, and he added that *I know mine, and mine know me.* When he says, *I know mine,* he means "I love them"; *and mine know me means* "those who love me are obedient to me." Dearly beloved, you have heard the danger I am in as a shepherd. Consider in the Lord's words your own danger. Are you his sheep? Do you recognize him? Do you know the light of truth? When I say "know" I don't mean by faith, but by love; when I say "know" I don't mean by your belief, but by your actions.

John, the evangelist who has spoken these words to us in his gospel, testifies that *he who says that he knows God and does not observe his commandments is a liar.* And so the Lord immediately adds here: *Just as the Father knows me, and I recognize the Father and lay down my life for my sheep.* He means: "This is what makes it clear that I know the Father and am known by him, that I lay down my life for my sheep. By the love which leads me to die on behalf of the sheep, I show how much I love the Father."

35 ✛ SALT OF THE EARTH

We must all of us strive zealously to make known to the church both the dreadfulness of the coming judgment and the kingdom of heaven's delight. Those who are not in a position to address a large assembly should instruct individuals, offering instruction in personal talks; they should try to serve those around them through simple encouragement.

Let us bear in mind what was said to the apostles, and by the apostles to us: *You are the salt of the earth.* If we are salt, we should season the hearts of believers.

You who are pastors, consider that you are pasturing God's flock. We often see a block of salt put out for animals to lick for their well-being. Priests among their people should be like blocks of salt. They should counsel everyone in their flocks in such a way that all those with whom they come in contact may be seasoned with eternal life as if they had been sprinkled with salt. We who preach are not the salt of the earth unless we season the hearts of those who listen to us.

We are really preaching to others if we ourselves do what we say, if we are pierced with God's love, if, since we cannot avoid sin, our tears wash away the stains on our life that come with each new day. We truly feel remorse when we take to heart the lives of our forebears in the faith so that we are diminished in our own eyes. Then do we truly feel remorse, when we attentively examine God's teachings, and adopt for our own use what those we revere themselves used for theirs.

And while we are moved to remorse on our own account, let us also take responsibility for the lives of those entrusted to our care. Our own bitter compunction should not divert us from concern for our neighbor. What good is it to love ourselves if we abandon our neighbor? What good to love and strive to do good for our neighbor and abandon ourselves?

We must realize that our passion for justice in the face of another's evil must never cause us to lose the virtue of gentleness. Priests must not be quick-tempered or rash; they must instead be temperate and thoughtful. We must support those we challenge and challenge those we support. If we neglect this, our work will lack either courage or gentleness.

What shall we call the human soul but the food of the Lord? It is created to become nothing less than Christ's body, and to bring about growth in the eternal church. We priests are to season this food. Cease to pray, cease to teach, and the salt loses its taste.

The food of our God becomes bland, and so gives no pleasure to our Creator.

Such uselessness seasons nothing. We must ask ourselves whether anyone has ever discovered God through our words, repented after our reproof, abandoned destructive habits because we spoke out, or turned from greed or pride? What interest has matured from the talent we received from God and were empowered to invest? He told us, *Trade until I come*. God comes now, seeking growth from our trading. What growth in lives can we show as a result of our trading? How many lives will we bring in our arms to God from the harvest of our preaching?

But if we are negligent, does our all-powerful God desert his sheep? No: he himself will pasture them, as was promised through the prophet. All who are foreordained for life God chastens by the sting of conscience. Through each of us, those who live in faith come to baptism; through each of us they are blessed in our prayer; through each of us they receive God's Holy Spirit, as we impose our hands. They enter heaven—and we? Our negligence drags us down. God's chosen are speeded on their way to their home in heaven by our labors, while our wicked lives hurry us on to hell.

36 + PREACHERS

Our saving Lord, Jesus Christ, sometimes counsels us by what he says and sometimes by what he does. In fact his deeds are teachings, because when without a word he does something, he is actually showing us what we must do. He sent his disciples to preach two by two, because there are two commandments of love, of God and neighbor, and because there must be at least two in order for there to be love. Strictly speaking, we cannot love ourselves; love is possible only when we reach out toward another.

The Lord sends his disciples out to preach two by two to make it clear to all that no one who does not love another person is fit to preach. *He sent them ahead of him to every city and place where he himself was to come.* The Lord follows his preachers. Preaching comes first, and then the Lord himself enters the dwellings of our heart. Exhortation comes first, and Jesus, the Truth, follows it into our hearts.

Listen to what he said after sending out his preachers: *The harvest indeed is great, but the laborers are few.* I say this sadly: Though many crave the good news, there are few to preach it. There are priests in plenty around us, but seldom do we find a laborer for God's harvest. We accept the role but not the work.

My friends, ponder what he says next: *Ask the Lord of the harvest to send laborers to his harvest.* Pray for me, that I may be able to serve you as you deserve, that I may never fail to challenge you. Then, having been charged with preaching, my silence may not condemn me.

37 + PREACHERS' WAGES

Into whatever house you enter, say first, Peace be to this house. And if a child of peace is there, your peace will rest on it; if not, it will return to you. The peace you offer either rests on the house or it returns to you. There is either someone predestined to life who receives God's word, or, even if you find no one willing to listen to you, all is not lost, because your peace returns to you. The Lord will pay you your wages.

See how the Lord, who forbade his disciples to carry a pack and a wallet, allows them to provide for their needs and nourishment from their preaching. He tells them to *stay in the same house, eating and drinking what is there: for the laborer deserves his wages.* If our peace is accepted, it is right that we should stay in the same house, eating and drinking what is there. In this way we receive our material wages from those to whom we offer a heavenly home. Paul also accepted these things, as a minimum wage: *If we have sown what is spiritual among you, is it a great thing if we harvest from you what is material?*

The laborer deserves his wage. Nourishment is part of the wage for work accomplished. The wage for the work of preaching begins to come to us now, with the final payment, the vision of truth, to come to us in heaven. In this connection we should reflect that we are owed a double wage, one coming to us on the way, the other when we reach our home. One sustains us in our labor, the other rewards us at our resurrection.

The wage we receive now ought to spur us on to seek the one that is to follow. No true preacher ever preaches just for present pay, but accepts payment in order to continue to preach. Those who preach merely for payment here and now, whether in praise or in gifts, have surely deprived themselves of payment in eternity. But then there are those who yearn that their hearers should love the Lord and not themselves, those who accept material wages for their preaching lest they be exhausted by poverty: surely they have a reward in heaven, even though they took something for their needs on earth.

38   +   LAMBS AMONG WOLVES

Our Lord said to his disciples, *See, I am sending you like lambs among wolves.* Many, when they are put in a position of authority, are eager to tear their subordinates to pieces, showing only the alarming side of power, and hurting those they are called to serve. So eager are they to be in control that there is no love in their hearts, and they forget that they are called to nurture others. They turn from humility to pride and dominance, and if they sometimes stoop to flatter those around them they are full of rage inside. Our Lord says of them in another place that *they come to you in sheep's clothing, but inwardly they are ravenous wolves.*

Against all this, remember that we are sent *like lambs among wolves*. Those who undertake the pastoral office should not be the cause of suffering but rather endure it. By their gentleness they can then allay the anger of the violent. Being wounded ourselves by ill-treatment, we can heal the wounds of other sinners. If our zeal for justice ever requires us to show anger, let it spring from love rather than brutality. Then discipline is honored, and we have in our hearts a parent's love for those we are chastising.

39 ✦ THE FIRST PREACHERS

Let us listen to what the Lord demands of his preachers when he sends them forth: *Go and preach, saying that the kingdom of heaven has come near*. Even if the gospel were to be silent, the world itself would shout this. Its ruins are words. It has been devastated on all sides, its glory has ended. In our own time the world itself reveals to us that another kingdom is near, another kingdom which will succeed it. The very people who once loved the world now find it abhorrent.

The world's ruins proclaim that we should not love it. If anyone's house were shaken and threatened to collapse, those who lived there would run. Those who cherished it when it stood would get away as fast as they could if it collapsed. If the world is collapsing, and our love clings to it, we are choosing to be overwhelmed by it rather than to live in it. When love blinds us to our bondage, earth's ruin is inseparable from our own.

It is easy, now, when we see everything heading to its destruction, to distance our hearts from the world around us. In our Lord's time it was very difficult. The disciples were sent to preach the unseen kingdom of heaven at the very time when everyone far and wide could see the realms of the earth flourishing. For this reason the preachers of his word were granted the gift of working miracles. The power they wielded was to lend credence to their words. Those who preached something new were to perform something new, as the gospel itself says when the disciples were told to *cure the sick, to raise the dead, to cleanse lepers, to cast out demons.*

With the world flourishing, humanity developing, the human body surviving ever longer, and riches abounding, who would have believed that there was another life, who would have preferred the unseen to the things they could see? But when the sick recovered their health, the dead were raised to life, lepers were cleansed, demoniacs were snatched from the power of unclean spirits—when so many visible miracles were being performed, who could not but believe all that was told of a world unseen? Wondrous miracles were done in order to draw the human heart to belief in what it cannot see, the far greater wonder within.

Today, as believers increase in number, there are many in the church who attempt to live virtuously, but they work no miracles. This is because a miracle means nothing when there are no hearts to change. That is why Paul said that *signs are for unbelievers, not believers*.

40 ✢ SIGNS

These are the signs that will follow those who are to believe: in my name they will cast out demons, they will speak in new tongues, they will pick up snakes, and if they drink any deadly thing it will not harm them; they will lay their hands on the sick who will recover.

My friends, since you do not perform these signs, does it mean that you do not believe? These signs were necessary at the church's beginning. For the faith of believers to grow it had to be nourished with miracles. When we plant trees, we water them until we see they have taken root in the ground; once established we stop the watering. This is why Paul said that *signs are for unbelievers, not believers*.

Let us take a closer look at these signs and wonders. Every day the church works in the spirit what the apostles once did in the flesh. When its priests lay their hands on believers through the gift of exorcism, forbidding evil spirits to dwell in their hearts, what else are they doing but casting out demons? And what else are we doing when we leave behind the language of the world for the words of the sacred mysteries, when we express as best we can the praise and power of our Creator, if not speaking in new tongues? When we remove malice from another's heart by our good word are we not, so to speak, picking up serpents? And when we hear the wisdom of the world, but choose not to act on it, surely we have drunk poison and survived. As often as we catch sight of our sister or brother stumbling on life's path, and we gather round them with all our strength, and support them by our presence, what are we doing but laying our hands upon the sick to heal them? Surely these miracles are all the greater because they are spiritual; they are all the more significant since it is the heart and not the body which is being restored.

My friends, by God's power you can perform these same signs, if you choose to. Such outward signs cannot bring forth life, but life can come from those who do them. Physical miracles sometimes demonstrate holiness but they can never create it, whereas the healing of the soul bestows life even if it is not evident to the senses. While even the wicked can do the former, none but the good can perform the latter. Hence Truth said that *many will say to me on that day, Lord, Lord, did we not prophesy in your name, cast out demons in your name, do many mighty deeds in your name? Then I will say to them, I do not know you; depart from me you workers of iniquity.*

My friends, do not love signs which even the wicked are capable of performing. Instead, love the miracles of love and devotion I have just described. The more hidden they are, the safer they are; the less glory that comes our way from others because of them, the greater our recompense in the presence of God.

COMMUNITY

LOVE ONE ANOTHER *
JN 13·34

The kingdom of heaven is said to be like a net let down into the sea. This net gathers all kinds of fish, and when it is full it is brought to shore where the good fish are sorted into baskets and the bad ones thrown away.

It is our holy church that is compared to a net. The church has been entrusted to fishermen, and draws all people out of the turbulent waters of the present age to the eternal kingdom lest we drown in the depths of endless death. It gathers all kinds of fish because it calls to the forgiveness of sins the wise and foolish, free and slave, rich and poor, strong and weak. The psalmist says to God, *Every human being will come to you!* This net will be completely filled when it enfolds the entire human race at the end of time.

The fishermen bring it in and sit down on the shore. Just as the sea signifies this present age, so the shore signifies its end. At the end of this present age, the good fish are to be sorted into baskets and the bad thrown away. Then all God's chosen will be received into their eternal dwelling, and the rejected will be led away into outer darkness since they have extinguished the light of the kingdom within them.

At the present time the net of the faith holds all of us, good and bad alike. We are mingled, like the different kinds of fish. On the shore is revealed to the church what she has been drawing in. The fish, when they have been caught, are unable to change; but we who are wicked can become good. Let us bear this in mind while we are still in the process of being caught, lest we be thrown aside on the shore!

42 ✛ FISHING

Twice in the gospel we read that the Lord told his disciples to let down their nets while they were fishing, once before his passion, and once after his resurrection. Before our Redeemer suffered and rose, he ordered them to let down their net, but did not say whether they were to cast it on the right side of the boat or on the left. When he appeared to his disciples after his resurrection, he ordered them to let down their net on the right side. In the earlier catch they took so many fish that their net was torn, but in the later, even though they took an enormous number of fish, the net was not broken.

You know that at the judgment the good are to be placed at the Lord's right side and the wicked at his left, and from this we infer the significance of right and left in Scripture. The first catch of fish, in which no directions were given regarding where the net should be cast, represents the church in this present age. The church encompasses both the good and the bad, and cannot pick and choose because she is ignorant of those she has to choose from. The later catch, however, coming after the Lord's resurrection, takes place only on the right side of the boat, because the gathering of the chosen at the end of time, when they behold God's glory, knows nothing of the deeds represented by the left side of the boat.

In the first catch, the net was broken because of the huge number of fish it took in. In the present age the ranks of the unjust coexist side by side with the virtuous in professing the faith, and in the process the church is torn apart with their heresies. In the later catch many large fish are caught, but the net remains unbroken. The church of the chosen continues in the uninterrupted peace of its Creator, with no dissensions to tear her apart.

43   ✝   THE GOOD AND THE BAD

The servants of the king went out into the streets and gathered all they found, both bad and good, and the marriage feast was filled with guests. The description of those present at the banquet shows us clearly that the king's marriage feast represents the church of the present time, which includes both bad people and good. The church is a thorough mix of a variety of her offspring. She brings us all forth to the faith, but she cannot successfully lead us all to spiritual freedom by a change in our lives because our sins do not allow it. As long as we are living in this world, we have to proceed along our present path thoroughly mixed together. Only when we reach our destination will we be separated. Only the good are in heaven, and only the bad are in hell. This life is situated between heaven and hell. We live, so to speak, in the middle, in the midst of people belonging to both. The church admits us all now, without distinguishing us, but she will separate us later when we leave this life.

If you are one of the good, you must put up patiently with the bad as long as you remain alive. If you refuse to do this you testify against yourself, by your intolerance, that you are not good. On the threshing floor the grains of wheat are pressed down beneath the straw. Flowers spring up amidst briars. A fragrant rose grows alongside a piercing thorn.

Adam had two sons: one was chosen, the other rejected. The ark contained Noah's three sons: two of these were chosen, and one rejected. Abraham had two sons: one was chosen, the other rejected. Isaac also had two sons: one was chosen, the other rejected. The patriarch Jacob had twelve sons: on account of his innocence one of them was sold by his wicked brothers. Our Lord chose twelve apostles: in their number was one who would put them all to the test, and eleven who would be tested. The apostles ordained seven deacons: six of them remained orthodox in faith, one became a source of error.[†] There

---

[†] Nicolaus (Acts 6.5), whom many of the Church Fathers supposed was the originator of the Nicolaitan sect (Rev. 2.6,15).

can be no bad without good, nor good without bad, in the Church.

My friends, before your time on earth is over, recall these examples. Strengthen yourselves to bear with the bad. If we are the offspring of God's chosen ones we must live according to their example. The good have never refused to bear with the bad. Job declared of himself, *I was a brother of serpents and a companion of ostriches.* Solomon, in the voice of the bridegroom, said of the church: *As a lily among briars, so is my love among the maidens.* The Lord said to Ezekiel, *Son of man, unbelievers and rebels are with you, and you live with scorpions.* Peter praised the life of Lot, saying: *And God rescued righteous Lot, who was oppressed by the lawless lives of the wicked; for he was righteous in respect to his sight and hearing, and lived among those who tormented his righteous soul day after day by their wicked deeds.* Paul praised the life of his disciples and encouraged them by telling them, *You are in the midst of a crooked and perverse people, among whom you shine as lights in the world, holding fast the word of life.* And John testified to the church at Pergamum: *I know where you dwell, where Satan's throne is; you hold fast my name, you have not denied my faith.*

You see, my friends, in all these examples how we recognize no good person who was left untested by the wickedness of the bad. If I may put it this way, the sword of our soul does not acquire a keen, sharp edge unless another's wickedness hones it.

44 ✛ GOD'S CHOSEN

When the servant of the man giving a great banquet returned and reported to his master that all
those he had invited had excused themselves, *the
householder in anger said to his servant, Go out quickly
to the streets and lanes of the city, and bring in the poor
and the feeble and the blind and the lame.* The proud refused to come, and so the poor were chosen. Why was
this? Because, as Paul said, *God has chosen what is
weak in the world to shame the strong.*

We need to look at the description of those who
are called to the dinner and who come. They are *poor*
and *feeble* and *blind* and *lame.* The poor are proud,
just as if they were strong, even in their poverty; the
feeble are those who are weak in judgment; the blind
are those lacking the light of intelligence; the lame
are those unable to move ahead in the right way.
These physical infirmities signify deficiencies of character. We see that just as those who were called and
refused to come were sinners, so these too, the ones
who were invited and do come, are sinners. Proud
sinners are rejected so that humble sinners can be
chosen.

God has chosen the despised in the world. Often
being despised recalls us to ourselves. The son who
left his father and squandered his share of the property came to himself when he began to be hungry. He
said: *How many of my father's hired servants have bread
enough and to spare?* He went far away from himself

when he sinned; he would never have come to him-self if he hadn't suffered hunger. The loss of all his worldly goods led him to begin to think of the spir-itual goods he had lost. The poor and the feeble, the blind and the lame, are called, and they come: those who are weak and despised in this world are often quicker to hear the voice of God, as they have noth-ing in this world to delight them.

45 ✦ FRIENDS OF GOD

I no longer call you servants, because a servant does not know what his master is doing. I have called you friends, because everything I have heard from my Father I have made known to you.

What is this "everything" he has heard from his Father, that he chose to make known to his servants in order that they might become his friends? Is it not the joys of spiritual love? Is it not the festivities of our heavenly home, which he reveals day by day to our hearts by his loving inspiration? When we love the things of heaven which we have heard about, we already know what we love, because love itself is knowledge. Jesus had made everything known to his disciples; he had transformed them from being lovers of the world, and they were on fire with supreme love.

The psalmist had seen people who were truly God's friends, and he exclaimed: *Great reverence have I for your friends, O God!* We can call a friend a kind of soul-keeper. Because the psalmist saw that God's chosen ones were remote from the love of this world, and were keeping God's will by observing his commandments, he was full of wonder at God's friends.

And as if we had asked him the reason why they were so precious he adds: *Sovereign power is theirs in abundance.* We see God's chosen subduing their own bodies, strengthening their spirits, commanding demons, radiant with virtues, and despising the things of this present life. They teach us of our eternal homeland by their words and their way of life. People can kill them, but never turn them away from it. That is why *sovereign power is theirs in abundance.*

You can see by the sufferings which led them to physical death the loftiness of their hearts! But are these great human beings few in number? The psalmist added: *I shall count them, and they shall be multiplied beyond the grains of sand.* Consider the world, my friends. It is filled with martyrs. We who look on them are not nearly as numerous as these witnesses to Truth. God has counted them, and they have been *multiplied* for us *beyond the grains of sand*, whose number is beyond anything we are able to grasp.

46 ✛ WORKERS IN THE VINEYARD

Our Lord says that *the kingdom of heaven is like a householder* who hired workers to cultivate his vineyard. Whom can we better take to be the householder than our Creator, who reigns over those he created, and governs his chosen in the world, in the same way that a master governs those who belong to his household? He has a vineyard, that is to say the church throughout the world, which has brought forth many saints like so many branches, from righteous Abel right up to the last of God's chosen who will be born at the end of the world.

In the parable the householder hired workers to cultivate his vineyard in the morning, and at the third, sixth, ninth, and eleventh hours. God's preachers have not ceased to preach from the beginning of this world up to its end: the morning extended from Adam to Noah, the third hour from Noah to Abraham, the sixth from Abraham to Moses, the ninth from Moses to the coming of our Lord, and the eleventh hour is from the Lord's coming to the end of the world. It was during this last period that the holy apostles, who received a full reward even though they came late, were sent out as preachers.

At no time, then, did the Lord cease to send his people workers to instruct them. When he first cultivated his people through the patriarchs, then later through the teachers of the Law, then through the prophets, and at last through the apostles, he was laboring at the cultivation of his vineyard, employing all these as his workers. Nevertheless, everyone who had right faith and good works, in whatever capacity or measure, was a worker in this vineyard.

The Hebrews are meant by the workers who came to the vineyard in the morning, and at the third, sixth, and ninth hours. The chosen among them eagerly worshiped God with right faith from the very beginning, never ceasing to labor at the cultivation of his vineyard.

The Gentiles were called at the eleventh hour, and the householder asked them: *Why do you stand here the whole day idle?* Those who neglected to labor for the whole of their lives, while so much of the world's history passed by, were like people standing idle all day. But consider their answer. *They said: Because no one has hired us.* In truth no patriarch and no prophet had come to them, and so their answer meant that no one had preached to them the way of life. But what are we going to say, to excuse ourselves for having ceased from good deeds? We have come to the faith almost from our mothers' wombs, we have heard the words of life from our cradles, we have received divine preaching from the breasts of holy church together with our mother's milk!

We can also apply these periods of time to each individual's life. Morning is the childhood of our understanding. The third hour can be taken as youth, because the sun is rising higher as the warmth of age increases. The sixth hour is adulthood, because when we reach our full strength it is as if the sun is in the center of the heavens. The ninth hour we take to be old age, because like the sun descending from its zenith, this age lacks the warmth it had in youth. The eleventh hour is that age we call infirm or old. Since one person is brought to a good life in childhood, another in youth, another in adulthood, another in old age, and another at the age of infirmity, it is as if the householder is calling workers to the vineyard at the different hours.

Consider, my friends, what you are doing, consider whether you are laboring in the Lord's vineyard. The Lord's workers are those who do not think of their own concerns but of the Lord's, who live lives of devotion and charitable zeal, who are intent on touching hearts, who hasten to bring others with them to life. Those who live for themselves, nourished by pleasure for its own sake, are rightly reproved for being idle since they are not striving to bring forth the fruit of good works.

Those who have neglected to live for God to the last have stood idle, so to speak, up to the eleventh hour. The householder calls even these. And frequently they are the first to be paid their wages, because as they are quicker to take leave of their bodies, they arrive at the kingdom before those who appear to have been called in their childhood. Did not the thief come at the eleventh hour? He confessed God on the cross, and gave forth his last breath almost as he spoke. The householder began paying the denarius *beginning with the last* when he called the thief to the repose of paradise before he called Peter.

THE
INCARNATION

ARE YOU HE WHO IS
TO COME * MT 11·3

Why was it that the world was being enrolled just before our Lord's birth except to show that he was coming as a human to enroll his chosen in eternity? It was appropriate that he was born in Bethlehem. Bethlehem is translated "House of Bread," and Jesus would say that *I am the living bread who came down from heaven.* The one who was going to nourish the hearts of his chosen with spiritual food was appearing in the flesh. And Jesus was not born in his parents' house. He was born away from home to show that by the human nature he had taken to himself, it was as if he was being born in a foreign place. I don't say "foreign" with reference to his faculties but to his nature. Of his faculties it is said that *he came among his own*; in his own nature he was born before there was any time, in our nature he came in a moment of time. The place where Jesus came, appearing as a being of time even while he remained eternal, is truly foreign.

The prophet said that *all flesh is grass.* Our Lord, when he becomes a human being, changes the grass of our flesh into wheat, and says of himself that *unless the grain of wheat falls into the earth and dies, it remains alone.* Hence he was laid in a manger, so that he could nourish all believers, all holy living beings, with his body, and we would not remain empty of the food of everlasting knowledge.

What does it mean that an angel appeared to the shepherds as they kept watch, and that the brightness of God shone round about them? Surely it means that those who keep careful watch over their flocks are worthy above all others to see the most exalted things, and that while they are watching devotedly over their flocks, divine grace shines more profusely upon them?

An angel proclaims that a king has been born, and choirs of angels join their voices to his. Rejoicing with him they cry out: *Glory to God in the highest, and peace on earth to people of good will!* Before our Redeemer's birth in flesh we were at variance with the angels. Our sinning made us strangers to God, and his citizens the angels cut us off as strangers from their company. Because we acknowledge our king, the angels acknowledge us again as fellow citizens of theirs. Because the King of heaven took to himself our flesh, the company of angels on high no longer despises us. Angels come to bring us peace, putting aside their earlier hostility.

Before Christ's birth Lot and Joshua worshipped angels and were not forbidden to do so, but in the book of Revelation an angel restrained John saying, *You must not do that, for indeed I am one of your fellow servants, one of your brothers.* What does this mean unless it is that the angels no longer dare to scorn as something weak and beneath them the human nature they honor as above themselves when they see it in heaven's King? Those who worship the human being who is God no longer refuse to have human beings as their companions.

My friends, let us take care not to let anything sordid defile us. In the eternal foreknowledge we are equal to God's citizens the angels. Let us claim our dignity by our way of life. We should not let dissipation corrupt us or base thoughts find us out. Wickedness shouldn't gnaw at our minds or envy consume us like rust. Pride shouldn't make us swell up or the search for earthly pleasures devour us or anger inflame us. Human beings have been called gods! You who are human, protect the dignity of God that is yours against vice: for your sake God became human!

48   ✛   GIFTS OF THE MAGI

The Magi brought with them gold, frankincense and myrrh. Gold is an appropriate gift for a king, we offer frankincense in sacrifice to God, and we embalm the bodies of our dead with myrrh. With their mystical gifts the Magi are making known the one they worship: by the gold that he is a king, by the frankincense that he is God, and by the myrrh that he is a human being.

There are some people who believe that Jesus is God, but do not believe that he is sovereign everywhere. These people offer him frankincense, but they are unwilling to offer him gold as well. There are some who esteem him as a king but deny that he is

God. They offer him gold, but are unwilling to offer him frankincense. And there are some who affirm that he is both God and king, but deny that he took mortal flesh to himself. These people are certainly offering him gold and frankincense, but they are unwilling to offer him the myrrh which represents the mortal nature he assumed.

We too, like the Magi, must offer gold to our new-born Lord to affirm that he is sovereign everywhere; we must offer frankincense, that we may believe that the one who appeared in time existed as God before time; we must offer myrrh, that we may believe that the one we admit was unable to suffer in his divinity was also subject to death in our flesh.

But we are able to interpret the gold, frankincense and myrrh in another way. Solomon testifies that gold symbolizes wisdom when he says that *a pleasing treasure lies in the mouth of the wise*. The psalmist bears witness that frankincense offered to God represents the power of prayer when he says: *Let my prayer ascend as incense in your sight*. Myrrh indicates the death of our flesh, and so the church says of its members who are striving even to death on behalf of God: *My hands dripped with myrrh*. We too offer gold to the new-born king if we are resplendent with the brightness of heavenly wisdom. We offer him frankincense if in our zeal for prayer we enkindle our human thoughts on the altar of our hearts so that we are able to give forth a sweet fragrance to God. We offer him myrrh when we use the spices of self-restraint to keep our mortal bodies from decomposing from our dissipated lives.

49 ✛ THE FORERUNNER

The words of the gospel reveal John the Baptist's humility. His virtue was such that he could have been taken to be the Christ, but he chose to be seen as what he was: *He confessed and did not deny, he confessed, I am not the Christ.* When he chose not to grasp Christ's name, in his humility he became a member of Christ.

And they asked him, Are you Elijah? And he said, I am not. These words recall our Redeemer's words in another place, and raise a question. When his disciples asked our Lord about the coming of Elijah, he answered: *Elijah has already come, and they did not know him but did to him whatever they pleased; and if you want to know, John is Elijah.* John, when he was asked said, *I am not Elijah.* Is the prophet of truth denying what truth asserts? *He is* and *I am not* cannot both be true. Can John be the prophet of truth if he is not in agreement with the assertions of truth?

If we look carefully, we find that what sounds contradictory is not really so. The angel told Zechariah, concerning the promised birth of his son John, that *he will come in the spirit and power of Elijah.* This was said because just as Elijah is the forerunner of the Lord's second coming, so was John the forerunner of his first; as Elijah will come as the forerunner of the Judge, so was John the forerunner of the Redeemer. John, then, was Elijah in spirit; he was not Elijah in person. What the Lord spoke of the spirit, John denied of the person. The Lord offered a spiritual truth about John to his disciples; when John answered the literal-minded crowds, he spoke not about his spirit but about his body. What John said appears to contradict truth, but he did not depart from the way of truth.

Are you the prophet? And he answered: No. He also denied that he was the prophet, since he was not only to preach the Redeemer but also to point him out.

Then he declared who he was: *I am the voice of one crying in the wilderness.* You know, my friends, that God's only-begotten Son is called the Word of the Father, according to the testimony of the evangelist who said: *In the beginning was the Word, and the Word was with God, and the Word was God.* You know from your own experience of speaking that first a voice speaks so that afterwards a word can be heard. John declares that he is the voice because he comes before the Word. He is the forerunner of the Lord's coming, and is called a voice since it is through his ministry that we hear the Father's Word. He cries out in the wilderness because he reveals to an abandoned and forsaken Judea the consoling news of its redemption.

As for the subject of his proclamation, he says: *Make straight the way of the Lord, as the prophet Isaiah said*. We make the Lord's way to our hearts straight when we listen humbly to the words of truth; we make his way to our hearts straight when we order our lives in accordance with his teachings. The Lord told us that he and his Father would come and make their home with those who keep his commandment. Those who are proud, or avaricious, or dissipated, are shutting the doors of their hearts against truth, so that the Lord cannot come to them; they are barring the enclosure of their souls with their vices.

Those who had been sent to inquire of him asked: *Then why are you baptizing, if you are not the Christ, nor Elijah, nor the prophet?* The evangelist has just told us that those who had been sent were from the Pharisees, thus silently informing us that they were not asking from any desire to know the truth, but maliciously, expressing their envy.

But holy people do not turn aside from their pursuit of goodness even when questioned by a twisted heart. So John responds to these words of envy by preaching life: *I baptize with water, but among you stands one whom you do not know.* John was not baptizing with the Spirit, but with water, since he was unable to take away sins. He washed the bodies of those he was baptizing with water, but not their hearts with pardon. Why did he baptize, then, except to fulfill his vocation as forerunner? His birth anticipated one who was to be born; his baptizing anticipated the Lord's true baptism. His preaching made him Christ's forerunner, and he became his forerunner by baptizing too, making use of a symbol of the future sacrament. And along with these mysteries he makes known to us the mystery of our Redeemer. He declares that he has stood among us, and has not been known, because the Lord appeared by means of a human body; because God came in flesh, visible in his body, invisible in his majesty.

John goes on to say about Christ: *He who comes after me was before me*—*was before me* means "ranks before me." He *comes after me* because he was born later; he *was before me* because he has precedence over me. A little earlier in the gospel he revealed the reason for this precedence when he said *because he was before me*. John means that even though Christ was born after him, he surpasses him. The time of Christ's birth does not define him. He was born of his mother in time, but he was begotten by his Father outside of time.

50 ✦ CHRIST'S TEMPTATIONS

Some people are inclined to question what spirit it was that led Jesus into the desert, on account of what is set down in the account of his temptations: *The devil took him to the holy city*; and, *The devil took him to a very high mountain*. But our belief that he was led into the desert by the Holy Spirit, that his own Spirit led him where the evil spirit could find and tempt him, is true and beyond question.

When we hear that God incarnate was taken by the devil to a high mountain or into the holy city our minds shrink from it, and our ears cringe at the sound. But why should we be surprised if he allowed the devil to lead him into the desert, when he suffered himself to be crucified by those whose lot was with the devil? It is not unworthy of our Redeemer that he chose to be tempted when he had come to be slain. Surely it was right that he vanquished our temptations by his temptations, just as he had come to overcome our death by his death!

When we look at the progress of his temptations, we see how great the struggle was that set us free from temptation. Satan rose up against the first human beings, our ancestors, tempting them in three ways, by gluttony, vainglory, and greed. He tempted them by gluttony when he showed them the forbidden fruit of the tree and told them to taste it. He tempted them by vainglory when he told them, *You will be like gods*. He tempted them by greed when he added the words *knowing good and evil*. Greed is not concerned only with money, but also with honor. We rightly call it greed when we seek honor beyond measure. If grasping at honor was not related to greed Paul would not have said of God's only-begotten Son that *he did not think that being equal to God was something to be grasped*. The devil drew our ancestors to the sin of pride, then, by stirring up in them a greedy desire for honor.

The means by which he overcame the first human being were the same ones which caused him to be defeated when he tempted the second. He tempted Jesus by gluttony when he said: *Tell these stones to become bread.* He tempted him by vainglory when he said: *If you are the Son of God, cast yourself down.* He tempted him by a greedy desire for honor when he showed him all the kingdoms of the world and said: *I will give you all these if you will fall down and worship me.* But the second man overcame the devil by the very means the devil boasted he had used to overcome the first; and so he departs, defeated, from our hearts by that very same way through which he had gained entrance when he took possession of us.

And after the devil left Jesus, *angels ministered to him.* What else does this reveal but the two natures of his one person? He is both a human being, whom the devil tempted, and God, to whom the angels ministered. We must acknowledge in him our own nature, since the devil would not have tempted him unless he saw that he was a human being; and let us venerate in him his divinity, since angels would not have ministered to him unless he was God.

51   ✢   CHRIST'S MOTHER

The reading from the gospel, my friends, is short but weighty with mysteries. Jesus, our creator and our redeemer, is pretending not to know his mother. He represents that his mother and his relatives are not those who are related to him by blood, but those united to him spiritually. He says, *Who is my mother, and who are my brothers? Those who do the will of my Father who is in heaven, they are my brother and sister and mother.*

It is not surprising that Jesus calls those who do the will of his Father his sisters and brothers, since both sexes are included in the faith, but we may well be surprised that he calls them his mother as well. How is it that someone who becomes Christ's brother or sister by coming to believe can be his mother, too? We should know that one who is Christ's brother and sister by believing becomes his mother by preaching. Those who preach Jesus give birth to him, so to speak, by introducing him into their listeners' hearts; preachers become Jesus' mother if their words engender the love of the Lord in their neighbors' hearts.

Saint Felicity[†] is an apt demonstration of this. Today we are commemorating her birth into the new life of heaven. Her belief made her Christ's servant, her preaching made her Christ's mother. In the more reliable accounts of her life we read that she feared leaving her seven sons alive when she was dead, as

---

[†] A Roman martyr of the second century, commemorated in the Roman Martyrology on November 23. She is also commemorated with her seven sons on July 10.

other parents fear that their children may die before them. When her sons were caught in the persecution she strengthened them by her preaching, confirming their love of their home in heaven. She gave birth in the spirit to the sons she had borne physically; by her preaching she would bring forth to God the sons she had brought forth to the world.

I don't call this woman a martyr—she was more than a martyr. She sent seven pledges ahead of her to the kingdom. She died seven times before her own death. She was the first to come to the trial and the eighth to come through it. She was afflicted when she saw the death of her sons, but imperturbable. To her natural grief she joined the joy of hope. When they were alive she was afraid for them, that if one of them survived her he might not be with her hereafter. Don't think that she had no natural feelings while her sons were dying. She knew that they were her own flesh and blood, and she couldn't see them die without grieving. But she had within her a power of love that overcame her natural grief.

Peter too was to suffer. He was told, *When you are old, you will stretch out your hands and another will gird you and lead you where you do not wish to go.* Peter must have had some willingness to suffer for Christ. His flesh was weak, and made him unwilling to face martyrdom; but the power of the Spirit made him love it. His flesh was afraid of the sufferings he would endure, but his spirit was filled with exultation over the glory he would win. So it came about that he willed the torment of martyrdom, even as he was unwilling to face it.

We have an example of this in our own lives. When we want to enjoy good health we take bitter medicine to purge ourselves. There is no pleasure in the bitterness, but we will take pleasure in the good health it is to restore. By her natural emotion Felicity loved her sons: because of her love of heaven she willed that those whom she loved should die in her presence.

52   ✛   THE CRUCIFIXION

There comes to my mind what the bystanders said derisively of the crucified Son of God: *If he is the king of Israel, let him come down from the cross, and we will believe in him.* If he had yielded to their derision, and come down then from the cross, he would not have demonstrated to us the virtue of patience. Instead, he waited for a while; he endured their taunts, he bore with their mockery, he preserved his patience, he deferred their esteem, and he who did not will to come down from the cross rose from the sepulcher.

Rising from the tomb was a greater thing than coming down from the cross. Destroying death by rising from the dead was a greater thing than preserving life by descending from the cross. When the bystanders saw that he was not coming down from the cross at their derisive remarks, when they saw him dying, they believed they had prevailed. They rejoiced as if they had consigned his name to oblivion. But see how his name has increased throughout the world, how the multitude which rejoiced over his slaying now grieves over his death! They perceive that it is through his suffering that Christ has arrived at glory.

53   + EASTER

You have just heard, my friends, that the holy women who had been the Lord's followers came to the tomb with spices. They who had loved him when he was alive were anxious to show him kindness even when he was dead. But their action is a sign of something to be done in the church. As we listen to what they did, let us also reflect on what we are to do in imitation of them. If we, then, who believe in him who died, are replete with the sweet scent of the virtues, if we seek the Lord with a reputation for good works, then surely we are coming to his tomb with spices.

And the women who came with the spices see angels, because those hearts that make progress toward the Lord by their holy desires, along with the sweet scents of the virtues, behold the citizens above. But we must note that the angel was seen sitting on the right side. What does the left side signify if not our present life, and what does the right side signify if not everlasting life? Hence it is written in the Song of Songs, *His left hand is under my head, and his right hand will embrace me!* Since our Redeemer has now passed through the mortality of the present life, it was only right that the angel who had come to proclaim his everlasting life was sitting on the right side.

The angel appeared to them covered by a white robe because he proclaimed the joys of our festival. The whiteness of his garment makes apparent the splendor of our solemn feast. Ours, should we say, or the angel's? To speak truly, let us say both his and ours. Our Redeemer's resurrection is our day of great joy, since he restored us to immortality; it was also a day of joy for the angels, because by recalling us to heaven he has filled up their full number. At his and our festival, then, the angel appeared in white garments, since while we are brought back to heaven through the Lord's resurrection, at the same time the harm done to their heavenly home is repaired.

The angel told the women, *Do not be afraid.* Those people are afraid who have no love for the coming of the citizens of heaven; those are alarmed who are oppressed by the desires of the flesh and therefore despair of belonging to their company.

Then the angel says, *You seek Jesus of Nazareth.* The name Jesus means "saving," that is, "Saviour." However at that time many could have been called Jesus, not as indicating their nature but simply as a name, and so to make clear which Jesus he means the angels adds, *of Nazareth.* And then he supplies his situation: *who was crucified.*

And then he says: *He has risen, he is not here!* "He is not here" is said of the physical presence of one whose majesty is always present.

But go, tell his disciples and Peter that he is going before you to Galilee. Why, when he has mentioned the disciples, does he single out Peter by name? If the angel had not mentioned him then by name, Peter, who had denied his Master, might not have dared come among the disciples. He is called by his name so that his denial might not lead him to despair.

In this connection we should ask ourselves why almighty God allowed the one he had put over the whole church to be frightened by the voice of a serving woman and to deny himself. We acknowledge, of course, that this was done by a special provision of his great loving-kindness. He who was to be pastor of the church was to learn though his own failure how compassionate he would have to be toward others. First God revealed him to himself, and then he placed him over others. This was so that Peter might recognize from his own weakness how compassionately he was to bear the weaknesses of others.

The angel spoke well of our Redeemer when he said: *He is going before you into Galilee; there you will see him as he told you.* Galilee means "a passing over completed." Our Redeemer had now passed over from suffering to resurrection, from death to life, from pain to glory, from mortality to immortality. And his disciples first see him after his resurrection in Galilee, because if we now pass over from our ways of sin to the height of holy living, we shall afterwards see with joy the glory of his resurrection. He who was proclaimed in the tomb is revealed in the passing over, because he who is recognized in the putting to death of the flesh is seen in the passing over of the mind.

54 ✛ THE LORD'S BODY

On the evening of that day, the first of the week, the doors where the disciples were gathered being closed for fear of the Jews, Jesus came and stood in their midst, and said to them, "Peace be to you."

The first question that strikes our minds when we hear this reading from the gospel is how the Lord's body, which was capable of coming in among his disciples through closed doors after the resurrection, was a real one. But of this we can be sure, that a divine work that we can comprehend is not worthy of our admiration, and that our faith has no value when human reason provides a proof. We are to consider those actions of our Redeemer, which we cannot understand by themselves, in the light of other divine works. Then those that are more wonderful can lead us to believe in those that are more ordinary.

The Lord's body, which made its entrance among the disciples through closed doors, was the same body which issued from the Virgin's closed womb at his birth. Is it surprising if he who was now to live forever made his entrance through closed doors after his resurrection, when on his coming in order to die he made his appearance from the unopened womb of a virgin?

But the faith of those looking on wavered concerning this body they were able to see, and so he immediately showed them his hands and his side. He allowed them to touch the flesh he had brought in through the closed doors. By this action he revealed two wonders which, according to human reason, are utterly contradictory. Jesus showed them that after his resurrection his body was both imperishable and yet capable of being touched. What we can touch is perishable: it cannot be otherwise. What is not perishable cannot be touched. But in a wonderful and incomprehensible way our Redeemer, after his resurrection, manifested a body that was imperishable and yet touchable. By showing us that it is imperishable he intended to urge us on to our reward, and by offering it to be touched he intended to dispose us toward faith. He manifested himself as both imperishable and touchable truly to show us that his body after his resurrection is of the same nature as ours, but of a glory which is not ours.

55 + THE ASCENSION

My friends, on this solemn feast we must particularly consider that today the decree of our condemnation has been cancelled,[†] our sentencing to death has been changed. The nature which was told, *You are dust, and to dust you shall return*, today ascended to heaven. Of this festival the psalmist said: *Your splendor has been raised above the heavens*; and again: *God has ascended with a shout of joy, and the Lord with the sound of a trumpet*; and again: *Ascending on high he led captivity captive; he gave gifts to all people.*

Ascending on high, he led captivity captive since he destroyed our mortality by the power of his immortality. *He gave gifts to all people* because, *after sending the Spirit from above, he gave to one a word of wisdom, to another a word of knowledge, to another the gift of the virtues, to another the gift of healing, to another various tongues, and to another the gift of interpreting them. He gave gifts to all people.*

Of the glory of the Lord's ascension Habakkuk said that *the sun was raised up, and the moon stood in its place.* What do "sun" and "moon" signify but the Lord and his church? Until Jesus ascended into heaven his

---

[†] This phrase is from Paul's letter to the Colossians (2.14). In a note on the passage the Jerusalem Bible (1966) says, "In the person of his Son, whom he allowed to be executed, God nailed up and destroyed our death warrant, as well as all the charges it made against us."

church was filled with fear of the world's opposition; strengthened by his ascension, she openly preached what she had secretly believed. *The sun was raised up, and the moon stood in its place*, because when Jesus sought heaven, his holy church grew in the authority with which she preached.

And so the church speaks through Solomon: *See how he comes leaping on the mountains, bounding over the hills!* The church pondered the loftiness of his great works and said: *See how he comes leaping on the mountains!* If I can put it this way, by coming for our redemption the Lord leaped! My friends, do you want to become acquainted with these leaps of his? From heaven he came to the womb, from the womb to the manger, from the manger to the cross, from the cross to the sepulcher, and from the sepulcher he returned to heaven. You see how Truth, having made himself known in the flesh, leaped for us to make us run after him. *He exulted like a giant to run his course* so that we might say to him from our hearts, *Draw me after you; let us run!*

My friends, it is fitting for us to follow him in our hearts where we believe he has ascended in his body. Let us flee earthly desires. Let us no longer delight in anything here below, we who have a Father in heaven. We must take to heart that he who was mild at his ascent will be terrible at his return, demanding of us with the greatest severity what he has commanded of us with gentleness. No one should take lightly the time of repentance granted us. We must be concerned for ourselves while we can do so, because our Redeemer will come with great severity in proportion to the patience shown us before the judgment.

Reflect on these things, my friends, turn them over constantly in your minds. Disturbances in the world around us may still be driving your hearts to and fro, but fix the anchor of your hope in your eternal home. Establish your heart's attention in the true light.

We have heard that our Lord has ascended into heaven. Let us meditate on our belief. If physical weakness still holds us here, let us follow him by the steps of love. Jesus, who gave us our desire, will not fail us.

56 ✛ PENTECOST

Today the Holy Spirit came suddenly upon the disciples and completely transformed their earth-bound way of thinking. When the tongues of fire appeared outwardly upon them, their hearts within them were set on fire; while they received God in visible flames, they were being gently inflamed by love. The Holy Spirit is love, and so John says that *God is love*. Those who desire God wholeheartedly already possess the one they love; no one is able to love God without also possessing God.

If I asked any one of you whether you love God, you would answer me with entire confidence and complete conviction: "I do." But you heard at the beginning of today's reading the words of Truth: *If anyone loves me, he will keep my word.* The proof of love is its manifestation in our actions. That is why John says in his first letter that *one who says, I love God, and does not observe his commandments is a liar.*

And my Father will love him, and we will come to him and make our home with him. My friends, consider the greatness of this solemn feast that commemorates God's coming as a guest into our hearts! If some rich and influential friend were to come to your home, you would promptly put it all in order for fear something there might offend your friend's eyes when he came in. Let all of us then who are preparing our inner homes for God cleanse them of anything our wrongdoing has brought into them.

One who does not love me does not keep my word. My friends, enter into yourselves and ask yourselves if you truly love God. But we should not believe the answer our hearts give unless we have the testimony of our actions as well. We must examine our words, our thoughts and our lives concerning the love of our Creator. God's love is never idle. Where it exists it does great things; if love refuses to work, it is not love.

And the word which you have heard is not mine but the Father's who sent me. You know, my friends, that the one saying this is the only-begotten Son, the Father's Word. Therefore the word which the Son speaks is not his own but the Father's, because the Son himself is the Father's Word.

57 ✦ THE POWER OF THE RESURRECTION

There are some people who are uncertain about the resurrection of the flesh. I can be a more effective teacher if I face up to the questions hidden in your hearts, and so I must speak a few words about faith in the resurrection. There are many, like myself at one time, who fear that flesh and bones are not restored from the dust. When they see flesh decaying and bones being reduced to dust, they say, as if reasoning with themselves, "When is a person brought back from dust? When does it happen that ashes are restored to life?"

I answer briefly that it is far less for God to restore what once existed than to create what did not exist. Why is it so astonishing if one who in a moment created all things from nothing recreates a human being from dust? It is more astonishing that God created heaven and earth from what did not exist at all than for him to restore a human being from earth! But people notice the ashes of a corpse, and despair of its being able to return as living flesh. They are seeking to grasp the divine power with their minds.

They think these things because God's daily miracles have become commonplace through constant repetition. The entire mass of the tree that is going to be born lies hidden within one tiny seed! Let us imagine the marvelous size of some tree, and let us consider from what it began to grow into so great a mass. Surely we shall find that its beginning was a small seed.

Let us now consider how the strength of the wood, the roughness of its bark, the tree's taste and smell, its green leaves and abundant fruits, all lie hidden in that small seed. When we touch the seed, it isn't strong: where does the hardness of its wood come from? It isn't rough: what is the source of the roughness of the bark? Where does the taste of the fruit come from? And the odor of the fruit? The seed gives no indication of being green: what is the source of the greenness of its leaves? All these things lie hidden together in the seed, but they do not all emerge at once. A root is produced from the seed, a stem from the root, branches from the stem, and fruit from the branches. Another seed is produced in the fruit, and so we can say that even the seed lies hidden in the seed! Is it so wonderful, then, if the one who daily brings forth from a small seed the wood, leaves and fruit of a great tree should bring back bones, nerves, flesh and hair from dust?

When our minds have doubts concerning the power of the resurrection, and seek reasons for it, questions naturally arise. Questions ceaselessly arise, but still we cannot grasp the answers by reason. When our minds cannot probe what they behold by

sight, they can still believe what they hear concerning the promise of divine power.

My friends, think about what is promised. Ignore
the things that pass away with time as if they were already gone. Apply all your attention to hastening
toward the glory of the resurrection which Truth has
shown us in himself. Flee the earthly desires which
separate us from our Creator, because you will pene-
trate more deeply into the vision of almighty God the
more perfectly you love *the Mediator between God and
man*, who lives and reigns with the Father in the
unity of the Holy Spirit, God forever and ever.
Amen.

REDEMPTION

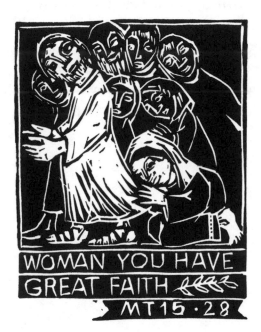

WOMAN YOU HAVE
GREAT FAITH
MT 15·28

Jesus Christ sometimes speaks to us through his gospel in words, sometimes in actions; sometimes in words alone, but sometimes in words which interpret his actions. You have just listened to two accounts from the gospel, my friends: the parable of the barren fig tree, and the story of a woman who was bent over double. The Lord exercised his loving kindness in both cases. He expressed it in the former through a parable, but in the latter by an action. The barren fig tree has the same significance as the woman who was bent over; and the fig tree was saved just as the woman was enabled to stand up straight.

A certain man had a fig tree planted in his vineyard, and he came looking for fruit on it but found none....Jesus was teaching in the synagogue on the sabbath, and a woman was there who for eighteen years had a spirit that left her enfeebled. What does the fig tree represent but our human nature? And what does the woman who was enfeebled and bent over signify but the same thing? Human nature was planted well, like the fig tree, and created well, like the woman. Of its own accord it fell into sin, and our nature preserved neither its fruitfulness in doing good works nor its upright stature. What was created in God's likeness did not stand firm in its dignity, because it refused to remain in the state in which it had been planted and created.

151

59 ✝ THE LOST SHEEP

The Lord asked, *Which one of you, who has a hundred sheep, if he has lost one of them does not leave the ninety-nine in the desert, and go after the one which is lost?*

See the wonderful parable of devotion Jesus has given us. Human beings can recognize its truth in their own case, and yet it applies in a special way to humanity's Creator. Because one hundred is a perfect number, God possessed a hundred sheep when creating the angels and the human race. One sheep was lost when a human being left the pasture of life by sinning. The Shepherd left the ninety-nine in the desert when he left the choirs of angels in heaven.

But why is heaven called a desert, unless it is because we call what we have left behind "deserted"? Humanity deserted heaven when it sinned; the ninety-nine sheep remained in the desert while the Lord sought the one on earth. Thinking beings, both angelic and human, had been created in order to see God. Their number was diminished when humanity was lost. The Shepherd sought on earth the one who was lost in order to restore the perfect sum of the sheep in heaven.

And when he has found the sheep, he lays it on his shoulders, rejoicing. He laid the sheep on his shoulders when *he himself bore our sins* by taking on our human nature.

And coming home he calls together his friends and neighbors, saying to them, Rejoice with me, because I have found the sheep which was lost. Having found the sheep, God returns home. Our Shepherd returned to his heavenly kingdom once humanity had been restored. There he found his friends and neighbors, those choirs of angels which are his friends because they keep his will unceasingly by their steadfastness; those who are at the same time his neighbors, because their constant presence brings them perfect joy at seeing his glory. We must notice that God does not tell us to rejoice with the sheep which has been found, but to rejoice *with me.* Our lives are his joy. When we are brought back to heaven, we complete the solemn feast of his delight. *I tell you that there will be the more joy in heaven over one sinner who repents than over ninety-nine righteous persons who need no repentance.*

60   +   THE LAMB OF GOD

There is a question we must ask, my friends. John was a prophet and *more than a prophet.* He pointed to the Lord as he was coming to be baptized, and said: *Look, this is the Lamb of God. Look, this is he who takes away the sins of the world!* Pondering both his humility and the power of his divinity, he said: *He who is of the earth speaks of the earth; he who comes from heaven is above all.* Why then, after he had been committed to prison, did John send his disciples to ask, *Are you he who is to come, or shall we look for another?* Did he not know the one he had pointed out? Did he not know who this was, whom he had proclaimed by prophesying, by baptizing him, by pointing to him?

We can resolve this question if we consider the time and order of events. John was at the River Jordan when he declared that Jesus was the Redeemer of the world; he was in prison when he asked whether he had come or whether they were to look for another. He did not ask because he doubted that Jesus was the world's Redeemer; he wanted to know if he who had come into the world was also going down into hell. His question meant: "As you stooped to be born on behalf of humanity, show us whether you will also stoop to die on our behalf. Then I, the forerunner of your birth, will also be the forerunner of your death; then I, who have already proclaimed to the world that you have come, will proclaim in hell that you are coming."

When Jesus heard John's question, he related the miracles he had accomplished by his power, and immediately refers to the degradation of his death: *The blind see, the lame walk, lepers are cleansed, the deaf hear, the dead are raised, the poor have the gospel preached to them. And blessed are they who take no offence at me.* Those who had seen so many signs and such power could not have taken offence; they could only have marvelled. Unbelievers, however, took serious offence at him when, after he had worked so many miracles, they saw him dying. And so Paul says: *We preach Christ crucified, an offence to Jews, and foolishness to Gentiles.* It seemed foolish to human beings that the creator of life should die on their behalf. People took offence at him when they should rather have considered themselves in his debt.

What did Christ mean when he said that *blessed are they who take no offence at me?* Was he not pointing to the terrible degradation of his death? It's as if he was saying, "Indeed I perform marvels, but I do not disdain to suffer miserably. Those who honor my signs must beware lest they feel contempt for my death."

61 ✝ SIN

Evil spirits may come even to the elect as they leave this life, seeking something of their own in them. Among all human beings there was only one who could say freely before his passion that *the ruler of this world is coming, and he has no claim on me.* Because the ruler of this world regarded Jesus as a mortal human being, he believed he could find something of his own in him. But the one who came into the world without sin also went forth from the world without any sin.

Peter was counted worthy to hear the words, *Whatever you bind on earth shall be bound in heaven, and whatever you loose on earth shall be loosed in heaven,* but he did not presume to say this of himself against the ruler of this world. Neither did Paul, who heard

the secrets of the third heaven before he died. Nor
did John dare to say it, who because of his special
love lay close to his Redeemer's breast at the last sup-
per.

For since the psalmist says, *Behold I was conceived
in iniquity, and in sin did my mother bring me forth,* no
one coming into the world with sin can be sinless.
That is why the same prophet says: *No one living shall
be considered righteous in your sight;* and Solomon says:
*There is no righteous person on earth, who does good, and
does not sin;* and John says: *If we say that we have no
sin, we deceive ourselves, and the truth is not in us;* and
James says: *All of us offend in many respects.* We can
be sure that the ruler of this world has something of
his own in the actions or the speech or the thought of
all of us.

But this world's ruler can neither hold us before
our deaths, nor seize us afterwards, since one who was
in debt to none paid death's debt for us. Jesus saved
us from having to pay our debts, and so we are no
longer in the power of our enemy. *The mediator between God and humanity, the man Christ Jesus,* freely
paid for us what he did not owe. For our sakes he offered the death of his flesh, which he owed no one, in
order to free us from the death of our souls, which
was our due.

Jesus said that *the ruler of this world is coming, and
he has no claim on me.* Let us take to heart, let us
ponder each day to the point of tears, how cruel and

dreadful we will find the ruler of this world when he comes on the day of our death to seek his own works in us. He even came to God in his flesh, seeking something in him, in whom he could find nothing!

What will we say, wretched as we are? What will we who have committed numberless evils do? What will we tell our enemy, who is seeking and finding much of his own in us? We shall say that we have one refuge, one firm hope; that we have become one with him in whom the ruler of this world sought something of his own and was able to find nothing! Christ alone is *free among the dead.* We have been truly set free from subjection to sin because we are united to him who is truly free. It is certain, and we cannot deny it: we have to confess that the ruler of this world has much against us. But even so, at the time of our death he will be unable to seize us because we have become members of one on whom he has no claim.

62 + THE LORD'S RESURRECTION

There are two lives. We know about one; of the other we are ignorant. One is mortal, the other immortal; one is corruptible, the other incorruptible; one ends in death, the other in resurrection.

The mediator between God and humanity, the man Christ Jesus came. He took upon himself the one life and revealed to us the other; the one he bore by dying, the other he revealed by rising. If he had promised resurrection of the body to us who knew this mortal life, but without revealing it, who would have believed his promise? Accordingly he became a human being and appeared in bodily form; he condescended to die of his own free-will; he rose by his own power, showing us by his example what he promised.

Someone may say that it was no wonder that he rose, since he who was God could not be bound by death. To instruct us in our ignorance, to strengthen our weak faith, he decreed that the example of his resurrection should not be unique. He alone died at that time, and yet he was not the only one who rose, for it is written that *many bodies of the saints who had fallen asleep arose*. And so Scripture demolishes the arguments of doubters. Lest we should not expect for ourselves what the God-man revealed in his own body, we see that human beings rose together with God; and let us not doubt that they were truly human beings.

If we are members of our Redeemer, let us believe that what occurred in our Head is taking place also in us. If we are greatly disheartened concerning ourselves, we must hope that what we hear of the first of his members is also taking place in us who are among the last.

63 ✛ SAMSON AND CHRIST

Samson, in the book of Judges, foreshadowed our Savior's death and resurrection, for when he entered

Gaza, a city of the Philistines, they immediately knew of his entry and quickly surrounded the city with a blockade, assigning guards there. They rejoiced at having seized Samson, who was extremely strong. But we know what Samson did. At midnight he carried off the gates of the city and ascended to the top of the hill.

Whom does Samson foreshadow by this deed but our Redeemer? What does the city of Gaza signify, if not the underworld? What do the Philistines represent, if not the unbelief of those who crucified him? When they saw that the Lord was dead and his body had been laid in the sepulcher, they assigned guards there. They were happy that they had caught him, the one who shone out as the Creator of life, and they held him behind the defenses of the underworld just as Samson had been held in Gaza. Samson not only went out at midnight, but even carried off the gates of the city: our Redeemer, rising before it was light, not only went out free from the underworld, but he also destroyed its every defence. He bore the gates and went up to the top of the hill, because by rising from the dead he carried off the defences of the underworld, and by ascending he passed into the kingdom of heaven.

64   +   THE CROWN OF REDEMPTION

My friends, we know what our teachers in the church were like before the coming of the Holy

Spirit, and we see how courageous they became after the Spirit's coming. If we asked her, the woman keeping the door of the high priest's house would surely tell us of the great weakness and terror that possessed the shepherd of the church, near whose holy body we are sitting now, before the coming of the Spirit. One word from a woman struck him down, and while he feared dying he denied life. Peter made his denial from the ground, while the thief made his confession on the cross.

Let us hear what this man who had been so afraid was like after the coming of the Spirit. There was a meeting of the council and the elders, and after beating them they declared to the apostles that they were not to speak in the name of Jesus. With great authority Peter replied: *We must obey God rather than men;* and again: *Whether it is right in the sight of God to listen to you rather than God you must judge. We cannot but speak of what we have seen and heard. And they left the presence of the assembly, rejoicing that they were counted worthy to suffer abuse for the name of Jesus.* See how Peter, who had been afraid of mere words, rejoiced at being beaten; how the man who had feared a woman's question before the coming of the Holy Spirit, after his beating scorned the power of the authorities.

How good it is to raise up eyes of faith to the power of this worker, the Holy Spirit, and to look here and there at our ancestors in the Old and New

Testaments. With the eyes of my faith open, I gaze on David, on Amos, on Daniel, on Peter, on Paul, on Matthew—and I am filled with a desire to analyze the nature of this worker, the Holy Spirit. But I fall short. The Spirit filled a boy who played upon the harp, and made him a psalmist; on a shepherd and herdsman who pruned sycamore trees, and made him a prophet; on a child given to abstinence, and made him a judge of his elders; on a fisherman, and made him a preacher; on one who persecuted the church, and made him the teacher of the Gentiles; on a tax collector, and made him an evangelist.

What a skilled worker this Spirit is! There is no question of delay in learning what the Spirit teaches us. No sooner does the Spirit touch our minds in regard to anything than we are taught; the Spirit's very touch is teaching. The Spirit changes the human heart in a moment, filling it with light. Suddenly we are no longer what we were; suddenly we are something we never used to be.

Let us reflect on the condition in which the Spirit found the holy proclaimers of our faith on this day of Pentecost, and what became of them. There is no doubt that they remained in the upper room out of fear. Each of them knew only his native tongue, but as yet none of them had ventured to speak openly of Christ even in the language they knew. The Spirit came, taught them to speak in a variety of languages, and made them strong of heart by filling them with

God's own strength. They began to speak openly of Christ, even in foreign languages, when formerly they were afraid to speak about him even in their own. Their hearts were on fire, and they disregarded the physical sufferings which they had formerly feared. They overcame their fear of physical pain out of love for their Creator. Formerly they had given way to their adversaries out of fear, but now they exercised authority over them. Since the Spirit lifted them to such a height, what can I say but that the Holy Spirit made the hearts of earthly people a heaven?

LAST THINGS

DO NOT LET HIM COME
SUDDENLY AND
CATCH YOU ASLEEP
MK 13·36

How often, my friends, have I urged you to flee evil works and to avoid the corruption of this world? Today's reading from the gospel compels me to say that you should also be circumspect about the good that you do, for fear that you may be seeking human good-will and gratitude. The desire for praise may creep in and deprive your outward deeds of their inner reward.

In Christ's parable there were ten virgins. All of them are called virgins, but they were not all received into the wedding chamber. Since within the church the wicked mingle with the good, the rejected with the chosen, we can say that the church is like the wise and foolish virgins.

The five foolish ones took no oil with them, but the wise ones took oil in their flasks with their lamps. Oil signifies glory; the small containers are our hearts in which we carry all that we think. The wise virgins have oil in their flasks because they keep glory within their own conscience, as Paul testifies when he says: *Our glory is this, the testimony of our conscience.* The five foolish virgins take no oil with them since they seek glory from others and do not have it within their own conscience. We must notice that they all have lamps, but they do not all have oil. Frequently those who are rejected have done good deeds, just like the chosen, but only those who look for inner glory from their outward works come to the bridegroom with oil.

When the bridegroom was delayed, they all slumbered and slept. While the Judge delays his coming for the final judgment, both the chosen and the rejected slumber in the sleep of death. *At midnight a cry arose: See, the bridegroom is coming; go out to meet him!* The cry arose at midnight because the day of judgment approaches so silently that we cannot foresee its coming. So it is written: *The day of the Lord will come like a thief in the night.*

Then all the virgins arise: both the chosen and the rejected are awakened from death's sleep. They all trim their lamps, counting the deeds for which they expect to receive everlasting happiness. But the lamps of the foolish virgins go out, because their deeds, which shine with an external brightness before everyone at the Judge's coming, are dark within. They receive no reward from God because they have already received the human praise they cherished. What does it mean that they ask for oil from the wise virgins? It means that at the Judge's arrival they want witnesses on their behalf since they are empty within. It is as if they say to their neighbors on finding that their confidence is delusive, "We are being rejected as if we have done no good deeds. You've seen our deeds! Speak up!"

The wise virgins say in reply, *Perhaps there will not be enough for us and for you.* On that day, our testimony will scarcely be sufficient for ourselves, so how much less for our neighbor too?

The wise virgins then admonish the foolish: *Go rather to those who sell, and buy for yourselves.* Those who sell oil are the obsequious. When they receive any kind of favor, they make a great deal of it by their empty praises as if they were selling oil. The psalmist says of this oil, *But let the oil of the sinner not anoint my head.* The oil of a sinner anoints the head when the good-will of an obsequious person softens our minds.

But when they went to buy, the bridegroom came. While they are seeking testimony to their good deeds from among their neighbors, the Judge comes, he who searches not only deeds but also hearts. *Those who were ready entered with him to the marriage, and the door was closed.* Can you who are listening to me feel within you the wonder of the words, *the bridegroom came*; the sweetness of *they entered with him to the marriage*; the bitterness of *the door was closed*?

Therefore be watchful, because you do not know the day or the hour. Since God accepts repentance after sin, if we knew at what time we were to depart from this world we would be able to select a season for pleasure and another for repentance. But God, who has promised pardon to every repentant sinner, has not promised us tomorrow. Therefore we must always dread the final day, which we can never foresee. This very day, as I speak to you, this day is a day of truce, a day for conversion. And yet we refuse to cry over the evil we have done! Not only do we not weep for the sins we have committed, we even add to them! If some disease should strike us, and its symptoms show us that our death is near, we would ask for a truce while we were still living, to weep for our sins; yet as we beg for a remission with great fervor and desire, we ignore what God has offered us.

66 ✦ THE JUDGMENT

Our Lord's words, *Many are called, but few are chosen*, truly fill us with dread. All of us have been called, all of us have come to the marriage feast of heaven's king. We believe and we confess the mystery of Christ's incarnation. We share in the banquet of the divine word. The King is going to come in on the day of judgment. We know we have been called: we do not know whether we have been chosen.

We must all humble ourselves to the degree that we do not know whether or not we have been chosen. Some of us never begin anything good; some of us do not persist in the good we have begun. We see one person who spends almost an entire lifetime in wickedness, but is called back from it toward the end by sorrow and deep repentance. Another seems to be leading the life of one of God's chosen, but toward the end turns aside into wickedness. One makes a good start and a better ending; another plunges into evil at an early age, and finishes in the same, becoming worse and worse. We must all be anxious and fearful for ourselves the more ignorant we are of what is in store for us, because—it has to be said often and we must not forget it—*many are called, but few are chosen.*

I say these things so that if we are now occupied in good deeds, we may not attribute the strength with which we do them to ourselves. We must not count on ourselves, because even if we know what kind of person we are today, we do not know what we will be tomorrow. We must none of us rejoice in the security of our good deeds. As long as we are still experiencing the uncertainties of this life, we do not know what end may follow.

I want to tell you of a recent event in order to comfort your anxious hearts with a story of divine compassion. Two years ago a certain brother came by the grace of conversion to my monastery, which is situated beside the church of the blessed martyrs John and Paul. He was tested according to the rule, and eventually received into the community. His brother followed him into the monastery, not from any desire for conversion but out of natural affection for his brother.

Now the one who had come to lead the monastic life was most agreeable to the brothers, but his brother was very different in his life and habits. He lived in the monastery from necessity rather than of his own free will. Although he was unruly in all his actions, everyone bore with him for his brother's sake. He was frivolous in his speech, misguided in his actions, careful about his dress but careless about his life. He could not bear it if anyone spoke to him of monastic life. He was a burden to all the brothers, but, as I said, they all put up with him for the sake of his brother. He was scornful if anyone spoke to him about his bad behavior, and he declared that he would never live the monastic life.

In the epidemic that recently killed a large number of people in this city, he was infected and came close to death. When the brothers saw that his end was near, they gathered to pray for him. Suddenly he began to cry out with all the strength he could muster, interrupting the prayers of the brothers standing about him, saying: "Get away from me! I've been given up to a dragon to be devoured, but it cannot devour me because of your presence. My head is already in its mouth! Let it be! Stop torturing me and let it finish me off! If I've been given up to it to be devoured, why hold it back?"

The brothers said to him, "What are you saying, brother? Make the sign of the cross!" He answered as well as he could, "I want to sign myself, but I can't because the dragon prevents me." When the brothers heard this they fell prostrate on the ground, and with tears began to pray more urgently for his release. And suddenly the sick man became better! He began to rejoice with all the strength he had: "Thanks be to God! See, the dragon which came to devour me has fled, driven away by your prayers! Now intercede for me, because I am ready to be converted and to abandon completely my worldly way of life."

And so this man, who was all but dead, was restored to life, and he turned with his whole heart to God. Instructed by long and continuous suffering during his sickness, he died a few days later. This time he saw no dragon as he died because he had slain it by his change of heart.

None of us knows what may happen in the hidden judgment of God, because *many are called, but few are chosen.* Since we cannot be certain whether or not we are chosen, it remains that we all should be anxious about what we have done, while rejoicing in God's compassion alone. We must not trust to our own virtues. There is one who can make our confidence strong, the one who deigned to take upon himself our nature, who lives and reigns with the Father in the unity of the Holy Spirit, God for ever and ever. Amen

67 ✛ THE WORLD'S ENDING

Just before today's passage from the gospel, our Lord says that *nation will rise against nation, and kingdom against kingdom; there will be great earthquakes in various places, and pestilence and famine.* Then comes what we have just read: *There will be signs in sun and moon and stars, and on the earth distress of nations, confused by the roaring of the sea and the waves.* Some of these things we see already, and we dread the coming of the rest. We see nation rising against nation, and the distress that follows on earth; it is worse in our day than anything we have read about in books. You know how often we have heard from other parts of the world of earthquakes destroying countless cities; we suffer pestilence without relief; we do not yet clearly see the signs in the sun and moon and stars, but changes in the air lead us to think that these too are not far off. There is no new turbulence in the sea and waves. But when so many of the things foretold have already happened, who can doubt that the few that remain will follow. The accomplishment of things past is a clear indication of what is to come.

I am saying these things so that your hearts will be watchful and disposed to be cautious, so that they will not grow lax out of a sense of security, and listless out of ignorance. I want fear to keep them alert, and alertness to strengthen them in doing good, as they ponder what our Redeemer speaks of next: *People overcome with fear and foreboding of what is coming on the whole world; for the powers of heaven will be moved.* What does our Lord mean by *the powers of heaven?* He means the bands of angels, archangels, thrones, dominions, rulers, and powers. At our Judge's coming they will appear before our eyes and we will see them: they will demand from us an exact account of all the things our unseen Creator patiently tolerates.

And then they will see the Son of man coming on the clouds with great authority and majesty. In other words, they are going to see in power and majesty the One they chose not to listen to when he was with us in humility. And they will find his strength more un-yielding to the extent their hearts do not now give way before his patience.

These things he has said of the rejected. Immedi-ately he adds words of consolation for the chosen: *When these things begin to take place, look up and lift up your heads, because your redemption is coming near.* Truth is encouraging his chosen by saying that when disasters grow more frequent, when the powers of na-ture bring terror, we are to lift up our heads! Our hearts are to exult! The world is not our friend. As the world approaches its end, the redemption we have sought is drawing near. In holy Scripture "head" often means "mind," because just as the head controls our members, so the mind organizes our thoughts. To lift up our heads is to direct our minds to the joys of our heavenly home.

We who love God are being told to rejoice and be merry at the world's ending. Soon we will find the One we love, while what we have no love for is pass-ing away. Why should we, who long to see God, grieve over the disasters of the world when we know that these disasters are going to bring it to an end? It is written that *whoever wishes to be a friend of this world makes himself an enemy of God.* Those who fail to rejoice as the end of the world approaches testify that they are its friend, and this convicts them of being God's enemies. This should not be true of the faithful, not true of those whose faith assures them that there is another life, and whose activities reveal their love for it. To grieve at the destruction of the world suits those whose hearts are rooted in the love of it, those who fail to seek the life to come, who do not even realize that there is a life to come. We who acknowledge the lasting joys of our heavenly home should hasten there with all speed; we should set out for it as soon as we can, and go there by the shortest route. What evils does the world escape? What sorrows and adversities are spared us? What is our mortal life except a journey? Consider what it is to grow weary with the exertions of the journey, and yet be unwilling to have it come to an end!

68 ✝ WORLD'S END

Truly, I say to you, this generation will not pass away until all has taken place. Heaven and earth will pass away, but my words will not pass away. No material thing is more lasting than the heavens and the earth, and nothing passes away as quickly as a word. A word, while it is incomplete, is not a word; but neither is it a word when it is completed, because it only becomes complete by passing away. The Lord means that nothing in the world that appears to last can remain forever without change, whereas what we perceive in him as passing away does remain. He means that his word, which passes away, expresses thoughts that endure without change.

My friends, the words of the gospel are now clear. New and growing evils oppress us every day. So few of us remain out of a countless people, and yet scourges continue to oppress us, sudden disasters crush us, new and unforeseen misfortunes afflict us. In youth our bodies are vigorous, our chests strong and healthy, our backs straight, our arms muscular; in later years our bodies are bent, our necks scrawny and withered, our chests oppressed by difficulty in breathing, our strength weakened, our speech interrupted by wheezing. So too was the world strong in its early years, as in its youth: lusty in begetting offspring for the human race, green in its physical health, teeming with a wealth of resources. Now it is weighed down by old age; as troubles increase it is oppressed, as if by the nearness of its demise.

Therefore, my friends, do not love what you see cannot exist much longer. Keep in mind Saint John's precept, in which he counsels us *not to love the world or the things in the world, because if anyone loves the world the love of the Father is not in him.* The day before yesterday you heard that a sudden storm uprooted an old orchard, that homes were destroyed and churches knocked off their foundations. How many people who were safe and unharmed in the evening, who were planning what they would do the next day, died suddenly that night?

69 ✛ OUR LAST END

We have read Christ's words in which he foretells the overthrow of Jerusalem. But Jerusalem has already been overthrown, and transformed into something better by its overthrow. The robbers have been banished from the temple, and the temple itself has been torn down. Since this is so, we must look for some interior likeness to these external events. The buildings overthrown must lead us to fear the ruin of our lives.

Seeing the city, Jesus wept over it, saying, Would that today you knew. Jesus did this once when he proclaimed that Jerusalem was going to be destroyed, and he has not ceased doing it every day through those he has chosen, when he observes people who have adopted bad habits after they have been living good lives. He mourns for those who do not know why they are mourned for, those who, in Solomon's words, *rejoice in doing evil, and delight in the worst things.* If they recognized their impending rejection, they would mourn for themselves!

The gospel says: *Would that even on this your day you knew the things that make for your peace! But now they are hidden from your eyes.* Those who look no farther than the things that pass with time have here their own day. They have the things that make for their peace. When they enjoy the things of time, when they are heaped with honors, when they are contented with their material pleasures and feel no dread of any coming punishment, they have peace on their own day. But there will be another day when everything which now makes for their peace will be turned into bitter vexation. Then they will begin to be vexed with themselves for not dreading the rejection they are suffering, for shutting their inner eyes so that they would not foresee the evils that were to follow.

And so the Lord tells them that *now they are hidden from your eyes.* Those given over to the things of time, who are enfeebled by earthly pleasures, hide the coming evils from themselves. They shrink from anticipating anything which might disturb their present happiness. It is written: *On a day of good things be not forgetful of the evil.* And Paul says, *Let those who rejoice be as those who are not rejoicing.* If we derive any happiness from the present time, we are to enjoy it without allowing the severity of the judgment which is to follow be far from our minds. It is written: *Happy are those who are never without fear; but those who harden their hearts fall into evil.* The less fear we have now of the judgment to come, the greater will be our distress when it does come.

Christ's words, opposed to every kind of evil, instruct us unceasingly on every page of Scripture. Thus even now Christ is doing what the gospel says: *And he was teaching daily in the temple*. Truth is teaching daily in the temple when he subtly instructs us, his faithful people, to avoid evil. We are truly being instructed by his words when we fearfully and ceaselessly keep before our eyes our last end, in accord with what a certain wise man said: *In all that you do remember your end, and you will never sin*.

70 ✛ TALENTS

The parable of the talents in the gospel counsels us to bear in mind that we who have received something more than others in this world may be judged more severely by the world's Creator. When his gifts to us increase, our responsibility to account for them also grows greater. We must all, then, be more humble and readier to serve as a result of his gifts, as we see that we will be constrained to render an account of them.

A man set out for foreign parts. Before leaving he called his servants and distributed talents to them for carrying on his business. After a long time he returned to demand an account from them. Those who worked well he rewarded for the profit they brought in, but he condemned the servant who held back from doing good with his talent. Who is the man who set out for foreign parts but our Redeemer, who departed to heaven in the body he had taken on? This man who set out for foreign parts entrusted his goods to his servants, for he granted his spiritual gifts to those who believed in him. To one he entrusted five talents, to another two, to another one.

At the end of his parable Jesus added a general statement: *To those who have will more be given, and they will have more than enough; but from those who have not, even what they seem to have will be taken away.* Those who have love receive other gifts as well. Those who do not have love lose even the gifts they appear to have received. In everything you do, my friends, you must be vigilant about guarding love. True love is to love your friend in God, and your enemy for the sake of God. Those who do not have love lose every good that they have; they are deprived of the talent they received, and according to the Lord's sentence, they are cast into outer darkness. Outer darkness comes as a punishment to those who have fallen voluntarily into inner darkness through their own sins. Those who willingly enjoyed pleasurable darkness in this world will be constrained to suffer punishing darkness in the next.

We must take it as certain that no slothful person is safe from the consequences of receiving a talent. No one can truthfully say, "I have not received a talent, and there is no reason I should be forced to give an account." Even the very little that any poor person has received will be counted as a talent. Some people have received understanding, and owe the office of preacher to their talent. Others have received earthly possessions, and are under obligation to distribute alms from their property. Others have received neither spiritual understanding nor many possessions, but they have skills that sustain them: in this case their skills are counted a talent. Others have acquired none of these things, but they may have become acquainted with some rich person, and have received the talent of acquaintanceship: if they never speak to him or her on behalf of the poor, they are condemned for keeping back their talent.

Those who have understanding must not remain silent; those with an abundance of possessions must not be slow to show mercy; those with a skill must be zealous to share their craft and usefulness with their neighbors; those with an opportunity to speak with some rich person should fear being condemned for keeping back their talent if they do not intercede on behalf of the poor.

The One who is to come will exact from each of us as much as he gave. So that all of us may be free from anxiety about the account we must give for our talents when the Lord returns, let us daily consider what we have received. The time is now near when the One who set out for foreign parts is going to return. The one who departed far from this earth where he was born went away, so to speak, into foreign parts, but he will truly return. If we are listless in performing good deeds, he will judge us more severely concerning the gifts he has bestowed on us.

We must bear in mind the talents we have received, and be careful in trading with them. We must not let any earthly care deter us from our spiritual work. We must not provoke our talent's owner by hiding it in the earth. Let us be watchful before we have to render an account of our talent, so that when the Judge is here the profit we have made may plead for us.

71   ✛   RETRIBUTION

How great do you think were the temptations that Lazarus, a poor man beset with sores, bore in his heart? He lacked bread, and even more, good health, and in front of him he saw a rich man, healthy and enjoying his pleasures. He was afflicted by pain and cold, and he saw the other with fine linen and purple clothing; he was burdened with sores, and he saw the other man abounding in possessions; he was in need, and he saw the other unwilling to give him anything.

How much turmoil did these temptations cause in the poor man's heart! His poverty would have brought him enough pain even if he had been well, and his illness would have been enough even if he had had people to help him. But to test the poor man more fully, poverty and illness together wore him down. Moreover he saw the rich man making his way through life surrounded by throngs of attentive friends, while no one visited him in his illness and his need. The dogs who were free to lick his wounds show us that there was no one there to visit him.

By allowing the poor man, Lazarus, to lie at the rich man's gate God was able to make two judgments: the rich man who was godless could increase his condemnation and punishment, and the poor man who was tempted could add to his reward. The rich man looked every day on a person for whom he felt no compassion; the poor man saw one who was putting him to the test. Here on earth there were two hearts, but there was One looking down on them from above. God was preparing the poor man for glory by tempting him, and the rich man for punishment by bearing with him.

And it came about that Lazarus died and was carried by the angel to Abraham's bosom; the rich man also died and was buried in hell. The rich man in his state of pain, the one who had refused to have compassion on Lazarus in this life, from his place in hell asked him to plead for him. *In his torment he lifted up his eyes and saw Abraham far off and Lazarus in his bosom. Calling out he said: Father Abraham, have pity on me, and send Lazarus to dip the end of his finger in water and cool my tongue, since I am tormented in this flame.*

How keen are God's judgments! How strictly does he repay our good and evil actions! It was said earlier that in this life Lazarus sought *the crumbs that fell from the rich man's table, and no one gave them to him.* Now it is said that the rich man in his state of pain was eagerly longing to have Lazarus dip his finger into some water and let it trickle into his mouth. From this, my friends, we can draw some conclusions concerning God's strictness and severity. From his place in hell the rich man, who had been unwilling to give even a little food from his table to the poor sick man, came seeking a little water. The one who had denied him a crumb of bread came seeking from him a drop of water.

72 + GOD'S WORD

Keep in your hearts the words of God that you hear. The word of God is our heart's food. When we hear this word and do not retain it in our memories, it is as if we are taking food into an upset stomach: we throw it up. We despair of the life of one who does not retain nourishment. You must fear the danger of eternal death, then, if you do not keep the words of life, the nourishment that is righteousness, in your hearts

See how everything you do is short-lived. You are daily hastening toward the final judgment, willing or unwilling. Why then do you love what you are leaving behind? Why do you neglect what conveys you where you are going? Remember what the Lord said: *If anyone has ears to hear, let him hear.* Everyone there with him at the time had ears on their bodies, but when he said *if anyone has ears*, he surely meant "has ears of the heart."

Take care that the word which you have received remains in the ears of your hearts. Take care that the seed does not fall along the path, lest an evil spirit come and take the word away from your memories; take care that the seed does not fall on rocky ground, and produce the fruit of good works without the roots of perseverance. Many people are pleased by what they hear and propose to themselves to begin good works; but as soon as adversities begin to weary them, they abandon what they have begun.

In his explanation of this parable, Jesus says that riches smother. They smother because they choke our hearts by the constant thoughts that they arouse. When they prevent good desires from entering our hearts, it is as if they are cutting off the intake of the breath we need to live.

We must notice the two things Jesus links to riches: anxieties and pleasures. Riches overwhelm our hearts with care, and cause them to be dissipated by surfeit. Contrary to our expectations, they make those who possess them both wretched and insecure. Pleasure cannot coexist with wretchedness. At one time riches make us wretched, because we are concerned with protecting them, and at another time they weaken us by providing a surfeit of pleasures.

Good ground brings forth fruit by patience. The good that we do amounts to nothing if we do not also patiently endure the evils done by our neighbors. The more we progress, the more we find things in this world which are hard to bear. As our love for this present age declines, the adversity caused by this age increases. This is the reason we see so many people doing good and yet laboring under a heavy burden of distress. They are fleeing from their earthly desires, and yet heavy afflictions are wearing them out. But according to the word of the Lord they are bringing forth fruit in patience. When they humbly accept their afflictions, they are afterwards received into heavenly rest.

So the grape is crushed underfoot and becomes wine; so the olive is pressed and squeezed and, leaving behind its dregs, becomes rich oil; so grain is separated from chaff by being flailed on the threshing floor, and when clean it reaches the barn. Those who desire fully to overcome their vices should be eager to endure humbly their cleansing afflictions. The more the fire of tribulation rids us of our rust, the cleaner will we be when we come before Christ.

HOMILY
INDEX

The numbers in parentheses indicate the homily and its sections, and the columns, in Migne's *Patrologia Latina*, vol. 76 (Paris, 1849). The quoted material refers to Gregory's use of Scripture in the text.

1. PLEASURE (36,1-2: 1266ad).
   "Taste and see ...": Ps 34.8
   "A certain man ...": Lk. 14.16

2. THE TREASURE HIDDEN IN A FIELD (11,1: 1114d-15c). See Matthew 13.44.
   "Let them see ...": Mt 5.16

3. THE PEARL OF GREAT VALUE (11,2: 1115cd). See Matthew 13.45-46.
   "love is stronger ...": Song 8.6

4. JOY IN HEAVEN (34,4-5: 1248a-49a). See Luke 15.4-7.

5. THE SEARCH FOR GOD (25,2: 1190a-91a).
   "Upon my bed...": Song 3.1-4
   "My soul has ...": Ps 42.2
   "seek his face ...": Ps 105.4
   "My soul has ...": Is 26.9
   "I have been wounded ...": Song 2.5
   "My soul melted ...": Song 5.6

6. PERSISTENCE IN PRAYER (2,1-8 abridged: 1082b-85b). See Luke 18.35-43.
   "I am the way": Jn 14.6
   "your Father knows ...": Mt 6.8

7. PETER AND ANDREW (5,1-2: 1093ac). See Matthew 4.18-20.

8. ETERNAL PASTURES (14,4-6: 1129c-30d). See John 10.11-16.
   "He is our peace ...": Eph 2.14

"My sheep heed ...": Jn 10.27-28
"the door of the sheep": Jn 10.7
"Those who enter ...": Jn 10.9
faith to vision: 2 Cor 5.7

9. MARY MAGDALENE (25,1-2 & 5: 1189b-90c, 1192c-93a). See John 20.1-18.
    "a sinner in the city": Lk 7.37
    "her many sins ...": Lk 7.47
    "the person who perseveres ...": Mt 24.13
    "I know you by name": Exod 33.12

10. DIVINE COMPASSION (25,10: 1196ad). See Luke 7.36-50.
    She sat at the feet ...: Lk 10.39
    she sought him ...: Jn 20.11-18
    she who was sent ...: Jn 20.17
    look at Peter: Mt 26.75
    look at the thief: Lk 23.43
    look at Zaccheus: Lk 19.8
    look at Mary: Lk 7.47
    "Like newborn children ...": 1 Pet 2.2

11. SIGNS OF LOVE (33,8: 1244b-45c). See Luke 7.36-50.
    rigor of the Law: Exod 19.12; Lev 20.2,27
    "I do not will ...": Ezek 33.11
    "If a man divorces ...": Jer 3.1
    "I have given heed ...": Jer 8.6

12. REPENTANCE (33,1-4: 1239b-41d). See Luke 7.36-50.

13. THE KINGDOM OF HEAVEN SUFFERS VIOLENCE (20,14-15: 1168b-70b).
    "From the days ...": Mt 11.12
    the Law says: Exod 19.12; Lev 20.2,27
    "Today you will ...": Lk 23.43
    "fruits worthy ...": Lk 3.8

14. LOVE (27,1-4: 1205a-06c). See John 15.12-16.
    "Father, forgive them ...": Lk 23.34
    "Those who have ...": 1 Jn 3.17
    "Let one who has ..." Lk 3.11

15. PATIENCE (35,4-6: 1261d-63b). See Luke 21.9-19.
    "love is patient ..." 1 Cor 13.4
    "Love your enemies ...": Mt 5.44; Lk 6.27-28
    "your teaching is ...": Prov 19.11 (Vulgate)
    "Better to be patient ...": Prov 16.32

16. DOUBT (26,7-9: 1201b-02b). See John 20.24-29.
    "faith is the ground ...": Heb 11.1

17. BELIEF (29,1 & 3: 1213c-14a,1214d-15b). See Mark 16.14-20.
    "While Jesus was eating ...": Acts 1.4
    "As they were looking on ...": Acts 1.9
    "They profess that ...": Tit 1.16
    "He who says ...": 1 Jn 2.4

18. COMPASSION (39,10: 1300b-01c).
    "Whenever you did it ...":Mt 25.40
    "the way of a man ...": Sir. 7.36

19. RIGHTEOUSNESS (34,1-2: 1246b-47b). See Luke 15.1-10.

20. MARTYRDOM (35,7 & 9: 1263bd, 1265bc).
    "Are you able ...": Mt 20.22-23
    "Father, if it be possible ...": Mt 26.39; Mk 14.35

21. HOSPITALITY (23,1-2: 1182b-83c). See Luke 24.13-35.
    "It is not hearers ...": Rom 2.13
    "Let the love ...": Heb 13.1-2
    "hospitable to ...": 1 Pet 4.9
    "I needed hospitality ...": Mt 25.35

22. GOOD WILL (5,2-4: 1093d-94c).
    To Zacchaeus: Lk 19.8

30. LOVE AND HATE (37,1-3: 1275a-76c).
    "no one is crowned …": 2 Tim 2.5
    "If anyone comes …": Lk 14.26
    love even our enemies: Mt 5.44
    "What God has joined …": Mt 19.6
    "Husbands, love …": Eph 5.25
    "So will they bind …": Acts 21.11
    "I am ready …": Acts 21.13
    "I put no value …": Acts 20.24

31. GIVE FREELY (4,4-5: 1091b-92c). See Matthew 10.5-8.
    Simon the magician: Acts 8.18-19
    a scourge of cords: Jn 2.14-15
    "they keep their …": Is 33.15

32. A PROPHET'S REWARD (20,12-13: 1165c-67c,1168ab).
    "those who receive …": Mt 10.41
    "they have set out …": 3 Jn 7-8
    "I will make …": Is 41.18-20
    "we are the aroma …": 2 Cor 2.15
    "Your land …": Gen 3.18
    "Thanks be to God …": 2 Cor 1.4

33. CHRIST SPEAKS OF JOHN (6,2-6: 1996c-99a). See Matthew 11.7-10.
    garment of camel's hair: Mt 3.4
    "You brood …": Mt 3.7; Lk 3.7
    "the words of the wise …": Qo 12.11
    "the lips of the priest …": Mal 2.7
    only one talent: Mt 25.18
    bowls but also ladles: Exod 37.16
    "Let him who hears …": Rev 22.17
    Christ asks …: Mt 12.36

34. THE GOOD SHEPHERD (14,1-4 abridged: 1127c-29b).
    See John 10.11-16.

"all flesh is grass": Is 40.6
"You have not offered …: Ezek 13.5
"he who says …": 1 Jn 2.4

35. SALT OF THE EARTH (17,9-11,16-18 abridged: 1143a-48c).
    "You are the salt …": Mt 5.13
    "Trade until I come": Lk 19.13
    he himself will pasture them: Ezek 34.15

36. PREACHERS (17,1-3 abridged: 1139ad). See Luke 10.1-7.

37. PREACHERS' WAGES (17,6-7: 1141b-42a). See Luke 10.1-7.
    "If we have sown …": 1 Cor 9.11

38. LAMBS AMONG WOLVES (17,4: 1140bc).
    "See, I am sending …": Lk 10.3
    "they come to you …": Mt 7.15

39. THE FIRST PREACHERS (4,2-3: 1090b-91a). See Matthew 10.5-8.
    "signs are for unbelievers …": 1 Cor 14.22

40. SIGNS (29,4: 1215b-16b). See Mark 16.14-20.
    "signs are for unbelievers …": 1 Cor 14.22
    "many will say …": Mt 7.22-23

41. THE NET OF THE FAITH (11,4: 1116ac). See Matthew 13.47-50.
    "Every human being …": Ps 65.2

42. FISHING (24,3: 1185bd).
    once before his passion: Lk 5.4-6
    once after his resurrection: Jn 21.6
    at the judgment …: see Mt 25.33

43. THE GOOD AND THE BAD (38,6-7: 1285c-86d). See Matthew 22.2-14.

Adam had ...: Gen 4.1-5
The ark ...: Gen 6.10; 9.24-27
Abraham had ...: Gen 21.10,12
Isaac also ...: Gen.27.27-37
The patriarch Jacob: Gen 35.23-26; 37.28
Our Lord chose ...: Mt 10.2-4; Jn 6.71
The apostles ordained: Acts 6.5; Rev 2.6
"I was a brother ...": Job 30.29
"As a lily ...": Song 2.2
"Son of man ...": Ezek 2.6
"And God rescued ..." 2 Pet 2.7-8
"You are in ...": Phil 2.15-16
"I know where ...": Rev 2.13

44. GOD'S CHOSEN (36,6-7: 1269b-70a).
    "the householder ...": Lk 14.21
    "God has chosen ...": 1 Cor 1.27-28
    "How many of ...": Lk 15.17

45. FRIENDS OF GOD (27,4: 1206d-07c). See John 15.12-16.
    "Great reverence ...": Ps 139.17
    "sovereign power ...": ibid.
    "I shall count them ...": Ps 139.18

46. WORKERS IN THE VINEYARD (19,1-3: 1154b-56a). See Matthew 20.1-16.
    Did not the thief ..." Lk 23.42-43

47. CHRIST'S BIRTH (8,1-2: 1103d-05b). See Luke 2.1-14.
    "I am the living bread ...": Jn 6.41, 52
    "he came among his own": Jn 1.11
    "all flesh is grass":Is 40.6
    "unless the grain ...": Jn 12.24
    Lot and Joshua: Gen 19.1; Jos 5.15
    "You must not ...": Rev 22.9
    ... have been called gods: Ps 82.6

"the sun was raised …: Hab 3.11 (LXX)
"See how he comes …": Song 2.8
"He exulted …": Ps 19.5
"Draw me after you …": Song 1.3

56. PENTECOST (30,1-2: 1220b-21b). See Acts 2.1-4.
    "God is love": 1 Jn 4.8,16
    "If anyone loves me …": Jn 14.23
    "one who says …": 1 Jn 2.4
    "And my Father …": Jn 14.23
    "One who does not …": Jn 14.24
    "And the word …": Jn 14.24

57. THE POWER OF THE RESURRECTION (26,12: 1203c-4c).
    "the Mediator …": 1 Tim 2.5

58. HUMAN NATURE (31,1-2: 1228ac). See Luke 13.6-13.

59. THE LOST SHEEP (34,3-4: 1247b-48a). See Luke 15.4-7.
    "he himself bore …": Is 53.12; 1 Pet 2.24

60. THE LAMB OF GOD (6,1: 1095c-96c). See Matthew 11.2-10.
    "Look, this is …": Jn 1.29
    "He who is of the earth …": Jn 3.31
    "We preach Christ …": 1 Cor 1.23

61. SIN (39,8-9: 1298d-1300a).
    "the ruler of this world …": Jn 14.30
    "Whatever you bind …": Mt 16.19
    secrets of the third heaven: 2 Cor 12.2
    his special love: Jn 13.23,25
    "Behold, I was conceived …": Ps 51.5
    "No one living …": Ps 143.2
    "There is no …": Qo 7.21
    "If we say …": 1 Jn 1.8

68. WORLD'S END (1,4-5: 1080a-81a).
    "Truly I say ...": Lk 21.32-33
    "not to love ...": 1 Jn 2.15

69. OUR LAST END (39,3 & 7: 1295b-96b, 1298b). See Luke 19.41-47.
    "rejoice in doing ...": Prov 2.14
    "On a day ...": Sir 11.27
    "Let those who ...": 1 Cor 7.30
    "Happy are those ...": Prov 28.14
    "In all that ...": Sir 7.40

70. TALENTS (9,1 & 6-7: 1106ab, 1108d-09d). See Matthew 25.14-30.

71. RETRIBUTION (40,4-5: 1306ad). See Luke 16.19-31.

72. GOD'S WORD (15,2 &3-4: 1132ab, 1133ac). See Luke 8.4-15.

BIBLICAL
INDEX

Biblical passages are cited by the selection numbers of Gregory's homilies.

C OWLEY PUBLICATIONS is a ministry of the Society of St. John the Evangelist, a religious community for men in the Episcopal Church. Emerging from the Society's tradition of prayer, theological reflection and diversity of mission, the press is centered in the rich heritage of the Anglican Communion. Cowley Publications seeks to provide books, audio cassettes, and other resources for the ongoing theological exploration and spiritual development of the Episcopal Church and other churches in the body of Christ. To this end, it is dedicated to developing a new generation of theological writers, encouraging them to produce timely, creative and stimulating publications of excellence, and making these publications available widely, reaching both clergy and lay persons.

Be Friends of God

Rendered in colloquial English, these readings represent the best of Gregory the Great's reflections on gospel texts, and presents spiritual and psychological insights into our struggles with desire and addictive loves in the Christian life. Here is a helpful introduction for the modern reader to a wise pastor and spiritual director who urges us to discern the roots of our desires and follow those which lead to new life in God.